Rev. Dr. Nadine Rosechild Sullivan, Ph.D.

Passing the Baton:
Birth Control -
Precondition of
the Liberation
*of Women**

Rev. Dr. Nadine Rosechild-Sullivan, Ph.D.

* The ability to control when, or if, one bears a child has been an absolute "precondition" of the liberation of (largely cisgender) women and girls – from the cloister of the home – to a place in the public sphere. In this discussion, there is no intent to misgender any individual or group. No disrespect is directed toward any individual or group, no matter how they identify. Neither is any disrespect meant toward those who, for any reason, are not reproductively-fertile.

It should be noted that the author recognizes that language is steadily evolving and frequently unwieldy. However, as reproductive fertility *of the gestational kind* is at the heart of this discussion, this discussion is, and must be, based in *reproductive-biology*. By biological paramenters, this discussion must – *of necessity* – be both limited to – and inclusive of – those who are *reproductively-able* to conceive and gestate biological offspring.

The author recognizes transwomen as women. By extension, without malice, with no disrespect to the truths of gender identity – as the discussion of reproduction is not about identity – but about plumbing – for the purposes of this discussion, the terms "woman(women)," "girl(s)," and "female(s)," will be understood to be *inclusive of persons with a viable uterus and ova*, including: adolescents (pubescent cisgender girls and transgender boys), reproductively-able adults (premenopausal cisgender women and [some] transmen), and reproductively-aged gender non-binary and [some] intersex people – *with a viable-uterus-and-ova* – who are, thus, able to be impregated (with, or against, their wills).

Also, for purposes of this discussion, the terms "man(men)," "boy(s)," and "male(s)," will be understood to be *inclusive of those with sperm-producing-testicles*, including: adolescents (pubescent cisgender boys and transgender girls), adults (cisgender men and [some] transgender women), and reproductive-age gender non-binary and [some] intersex people – – who are *capable of impregnating* a person *with a uterus-and-ova*.

Again, this author respects gender identity, and has struggled with the present limitations of language in regard to this work. I beg your forgiveness if I have not met your mark. Still, this book is not about gender identity. Rather, this book focuses on the personal-as-political, life-complicating factor of *pregnancy* – for any person, of any identity, *with a womb capable of (planned or unplanned, desired or undesired, controlled or uncontrolled) gestation.*

www.DrRosechild-Sullivan.org
Nadines@DrRosechild-Sullivan.org

www.chestnuthillspiritualcounseling.com
rosechild@chestnuthillspiritualcounseling.com

ISBN-13: 978-0-9848226-5-2

Produced in the United States of America

1. Reproduction—Contraception. 2. Liberation—Women's Rights—
Reproductive Rights. 3. Women—Girls 4. Motherhood—Fatherhood—
Parenthood—Family Planning. 5. Paternity—Paternal Rights—Child
Custody. 6. Sexual Politics. 7. Abortion—Rape—Incest. 8. Sex—
Gender—Sexuality—United States. 9. Christianity—Religion—
Fundamentalism.
I. Title.

Lifting Consciousness Press
Philadelphia

ABOUT THE AUTHOR

Rev. Dr. Nadine Rosechild-Sullivan, Ph,D. is a diversity and spirituality expert. Her education and life experience give her a breadth of knowledge and wisdom about gender, sexuality, ethnicity, race and their intersections with spirituality.

Rev. Dr. Rosechild-Sullivan has thirty+ years ministerial and pulpit experience, and holds a Ph.D. in Sociology, with concentrations in gender/sexuality and race/ethnicity, and a women's studies certificate, from Temple University, and a dual Bachelor of Arts in Anthropology and Sociology, with minors in Writing, African American Studies, and Women's Studies, from Stockton University.

Dr. Rosechild-Sullivan teaches sociology at the university (graduate and undergraduate) level.

As a sociologist and public speaker, Dr. Rosechild-Sullivan is **available for seminars, workshops, lectures, focus groups or consultation to reduce conflict and resolve misunderstanding** around issues of sexuality, gender, relationships, trauma, self-confidence, religion, spirituality, and multicultural (ethnic/racial) diversity.

As an ordained (interfaith) minister and spiritual counselor, Dr. Rosechild-Sullivan is available for congregational addresses and/or individual, confidential, spiritual counseling sessions (*by phone and online*) to reduce personal pain, facilitate healing, and help you find clarity and direction.

Dr. Sullivan may be reached at:
www.DrRosechild-Sullivan.org
Nadines@DrRosechild-Sullivan.org
Facebook.com/Pages/Rev-Dr-Nadine-Rosechild-Sullivan-PhD/198930586828943

DEDICATION

I dedicate this book to all the girls and women*
~ of all races/ethnicities/cultures/and religions ~
~ of all national origins and global locations ~
~ of all sexual orientations and gender identities ~
~ in multiple times and eras ~
who have gone before us – and walk beside us;
who fought – and continue to fight – for the civil rights of
ALL disenfranchised girls and women* (gestationally-fertile and otherwise):

- To the (un-assailed) vote
    - (and the equal citizenship (with all others) that it encodes)
- To own (or share) property
- To primary, secondary, undergraduate, and postgraduate education
- To fulfilling, self-directed, careers beyond the cloister of the home
- To entrance to the ministry and theological professions
- To entrance to the other professions
    - o   (politics, medicine, law, and the varied academic disciplines)
- To egalitarian romantic and familial relationships of respect and joy
    - o   and
- To **the core essential of reproductive rights**
~ which alone ~
has empowered those with reproductively-fertile *gestational* biology
the opportunity to live lives in which
***Anatomy* is not the sole defining feature of their *Destiny*.**

* ~ * ~ *

**May we find our way forward to the social justice of fully equal
civil rights for every, living, breathing, human being.**

TABLE OF CONTENTS

Reproductive

Self-Determination

I looked out my window and down upon the dimly lighted city. Its pains and griefs crowded in upon me . . . .

Women writhing in travail to bring forth little babies; the babies themselves naked and hungry, wrapped in newspapers to keep them from the cold;

  six-year-old children with pinched, pale, wrinkled faces, old in concentrated wretchedness, pushed into gray and fetid cellars, crouching on stone floors . . . .

White coffins, black coffins,

  coffins, coffins interminably passing in never-ending succession . . .

  piled one upon another on another . . .

  the destiny of mothers whose miseries were vast as the sky.

*(On the death of a New York City woman
who begged for the "secret" of preventing pregnancy).*[1]

---

[1] Quote from Margaret Sanger. (According to Alex Sanger, Margaret's Sanger's Grandson: [Margaret Sanger's] mother [his great-grandmother] was pregnant eighteen times: eleven children, seven miscarriages, and was dead at age forty-nine. This is not an uncommon story in nineteenth-century America. [Sanger] became an obstetrical nurse. . . on the Lower East Side of New York, where birth control was simply not available for the poor immigrant women there, and she saw one too many women go to the back-alley for an abortion or self-abort with a knitting needle or a shoe hook or undiluted Lysol, and woman after woman literally died in my grandmother's arms, and she said "Enough, there's got to be something better we can do." PBS.org. The Pill.
http://www.pbs.org/wgbh/amex/pill/sfeature/sf_history_influences.html

1. HOW IT USED TO BE

In an upscale Italian restaurant, local to me, on the wall above the heads of customers hung an antique, blown-up, family photo. Central in the photo is a couple, seated – presumably also Italian. Behind them stand one set of older parents and an assortment of adults. Given the rules of patriarchal, arranged marriage, these adults may be presumed to be the paternal parents and the siblings, of the male, of the seated couple.

On the floor at the feet of the couple sit nine, stair-step children. The face of the seated male in the central couple beams with pride at his offspring, but in the woman's face – the light has gone out. In fact, in each of the women's faces standing around her (her mother- and sisters-in-law), there is no smile in any of their eyes, or on any of their lips.

To the left of that photo hangs another – a shot of great architecture. In it, stone cathedral spires stretch toward the skies. Able-bodied, muscled-males labor around its base. Two of the workmen pause, to beam up admiringly at their own handiwork.

In this photo, there are no work*women*.

Autonomy & Safety

Without some form of female-controlled contraception – without pregnancy-prevention in the hands of *the partner who may be impregnated* – a woman's[2] anatomy *may* indeed *be* her destiny.

If she marries or partners heterosexually, the number of children she bears, and the impact on her life and health is the crapshoot of her own, and her male[3] partner's, degree of fertility. Without access to (and consistent use of) female-controlled contraception, girls and women (here, and around the world) are at markedly greater risk of having their life trajectories, and personal autonomy, hijacked by unwanted and unplanned pregnancies.

In the long era before the creation of reliable birth control (and in areas with limited access to contraception today), few women (no matter their other demographics) entered higher education – or had the opportunity to craft careers of their own choice. Instead, marriage was(is), generally, the

---

[2] Again, here and throughout this text, woman(women)/girl(s)/female(s) will refer to all those with biologically-female reproductive organs – most specifically, a uterus and ova. This discussion is not about gender/gender-identity/sex-gender-roles, but about the biological capacity to be impregnated (with or against one's will) and to gestate an embryo/fetus (for hours, or months, or to term, with or against one's will). This biological-sex reality is inclusive of pubescent girls, premenopaual women, transboys who have reached puberty without sterilizing hormonal intervention, transmen still in possession of a viable uterus-and-ova, gender non-binary, and intersex people *with* a *viable-uterus-and-ova* – who are thus, able to be impregated (with or against their will).

[3] Again, as explained by the asterisk on the title page, for the purposes of this discussion, the terms man(men)/ boy(s)/male(s), will be understood to refer to all those with biologically-male reproductive organs – most specifically, live-sperm producing testicles. This biological-sex reality is inclusive of pubescent/adolescent boys, adult males, transgirls who have reached puberty without sterilizing hormonal intervention, transwomen still in possession of sperm-producing-testicles, and gender non-binary and intersex people with *reproductively-fertile testicles producing live sperm* – who are, thus, *capable of impregnating* a person in possession of a viable uterus-and-ova.

2

only way to keep oneself and one's children from starving.[4]

Historically, few women have had the opportunity, or the *desire*, to choose celibacy as a means of contraception. Instead, most women were(are) forced, by family and circumstance, to marry.[5] And married women were(are) expected[6] to service their men – to have penile-vaginal intercourse[7] – whether or not such sex pleased them, and whether or not they wanted to conceive more children.

As I ate my rigatoni and worked on this text, the face of that mother of nine kept cutting into my consciousness, bringing back another mother's unsmiling face, in another photo – one in which *I* stood, also not smiling – one of *twelve* stair-step children – seven of us standing around our seated parents' shoulders, four of us sitting on the floor at their feet, one so young he was still on our mother's lap – father's face beaming.

Eight of us were born before the advent of the birth control pill.

Ten of us were born before the Supreme Court ruled *that pill* legal to be prescribed to married women.[8]

All of us were born to a woman whose church[9] forbid her the use of "*any* 'artificial' means" of birth control (which church continues to do so to this day).

The only contraceptive choice they gave her was to not make love, with the man she loved, 2/3rds of each month (just before/during/and after

---

[4] Still true in much of the developing world today
[5] Heterosexually
[6] By husband, by society, and by their own internalized sociocultural beliefs
[7] Generally without male withdrawal before orgasm
[8] U.S. Supreme Court Griswold v. Connecticut, 381 U.S. 479 (1965)
[9] Roman Catholic

ovulation – AND during her period[10]) – *IF* he were kind enough to take her "No" for an answer.

As I knew him, my father *was* kind (not at all an abuser).

And as I knew her, I presume my mother didn't actually want to say, "No" to her much-loved, well-suited, husband.

The "Right-to-Life" Movement calls "Natural Family Planning" (*also known as the "Rhythm Method," because it involves repeatedly [rhythmically] abstaining from sex during a woman's monthly fertile period*),[11] sufficient to plan and space children.

So does the current pope, Francis, who has not reversed the "ex cathedra" ruling of Pope Paul VI in his 1968 encyclical letter, *Humanae Vitae*.

~~~

To quote my R.N. (registered nurse) mother,
    wife of my family physician/D.O. (doctor of osteopathy) father,
in regard to the "Rhythm Method":

"All thirteen of you were Rhythm babies." (Rose Marie Sullivan)

~~~

In my mother's face, in the faces of the women in the photo at the Italian restaurant, heavy with the burden of their own reproduction – heavy with the burden of bearing and tending child after child, single-handedly (while their men *"worked"*) – is the answer to the mystery of women's

---

[10] Along with birth control, sex during a woman's menstrual cycle is not approved by Roman Catholic doctrine and is forbidden by the Mosaic Law of the Hebrew Scriptures, in Leviticus 15:24; 18:19; and 20:18.
[11] Luker 1984

historic invisibility – the answer to why there are no work*women* in the photo of the ascending cathedral.

For the heterosexual (or heterosexually-married) woman (or female victim of rape) – who cannot plan, space, or choose not to bear children – there is no designing or executing architecture, no art or literature,[12] no place in history.

The realities of compulsory marriage – and heterosexual reproduction – without means for its control – account for a great deal of the historic disparity of power and accomplishment between women and men.

It is access to reliable, female-controlled, contraception that has changed the status of women in the developed world from child-bearing drudges to "self-sustainable economic units"[13] – opening the doors of education and the professions, of business and ministry, of law and medicine to women – on a trajectory aiming toward parity with men.[14]

Contraception (the right to, and access to, female-controlled contraception) is a precondition* of the liberation of women – and by extension – of their men.[15]

Without the ability to prevent pregnancy, no woman or adolescent girl

---

[12] See Virginia Woolf. 24 Oct 1929. *A Room of One's Own* (essay).
http://gutenberg.net.au/ebooks02/0200791h.html
[13] Gazit, Chana & David Steward. (dir.). 17Feb2003. PBS. *American Experience: The Pill.* WGBH-TV.
[14] Though, even for U.S. women – the gender wage gap, the statistics on violence against women, and the lack of social opprobrium and sufficient legal remedies for sexual assault, domestic violence, and child abuse – demonstrate that we have not yet achieved full equality.
[15] Men, too, may be burdened by fathering children with a woman they would not have chosen as a wife or as their child's mother, by fathering children before they are prepared to support and parent them, or by fathering more children than they can adequately provide for in regard to time, energy, and finances.

can be free of domination. Whenever and wherever contraceptive information and consistent access to reliable methods of birth control are not available, girls and women are not able to plan and follow their own life-courses.

In the developing world today, wherever contraceptive information and access are limited, women are not free.

When pregnancy cannot be planned or prevented (or early undone), a girl's or woman's life can be taken completely off course by a single act of voluntary – or involuntary – sexual intercourse. The girl/woman who wants to be someone, who wants to accomplish or make a contribution, who has a passion for a field of inquiry or for a means of self-expression, can be swept out of the competition.

Pregnant, or as the mother of young children, it becomes much more difficult, even impossible, to finish school, to obtain a higher education, to have the time necessary to practice a craft, or the concentration necessary to found a business. The mother of young children can be stopped, simply by that circumstance, from further academic and career pursuits – and even with determination – may simply be unable to get back to them for a decade and more – thus, consigning her to financial dependency on a husband or male relatives, and perhaps, thereby, even to abuse.[16]

Through pregnancy, while not always dominated (because not all men are abusers), even a First World woman can be made *subject* to the "rule of

---

[16] Even within the family, the financial purse is power. Women who cannot earn their own living or support their own offspring, are, of necessity, under the (kind or cruel) thumb of whomever houses and feeds them.

men."[17]

She can be pressured by partner/family/or the social order to marry a man she would not have chosen.

Chosen or not, married or not – through childbearing – she can be trapped by a man looking to control her; because he, like all fathers, has parental rights[18] – and through her love for her child(ren) – she can be bound to an abuser – for life.[19]

Through the mechanism of motherhood, her heart can be broken time and again if an abuser uses her child(ren) against her – either by alienating their affection from her – or by harming the child(ren) directly in ways she cannot physically – or legally – stop.

Enacted, in secret, behind closed doors, physical and/or sexual abuse by partners and fathers often cannot be sufficiently "proven" in court.[20]

And even when concrete evidence exists (medical examinations, reports by teachers and counselors, records of police calls for domestic or sexual violence), it still may not be "proven" in court – especially if the victim/victims' mother (deprived of a full education and lucrative career through early and/or repeated pregnancy) finds herself without sufficient money for the extensive legal fees necessary to find and hire a "good"

---

[17] Nazer, Mende & Damien Lewis. (2004). Slave: My True Story. Public Affairs.; Souad & Marie-Therese Cuny. 2004. Burned Alive: A Surviovr of an "Honor Killing" Speaks Out. Grand Central Publishing.

[18] Except in the relatively rare cases where they are severed by a court.

[19] Even when children are grown, an abusive man may continue to insert himself into a woman's life by his contact with and impact on her grown children, grandchildren, great-grandchildren, etc.

[20] With her testimony dismissed as "he said/she said," and children's testimony dismissed as "coerced" or "coached"

lawyer to successfully take the perpetrator to court.

Without contraception – *in social orders where women, en masse, have little to no access to birth control information or female-controlled contraception* – women can be (and are), en masse, denied access to higher education and self-determined careers.

They may work – selling their time for money – cooking and cleaning and taking in laundry, and taking care of the children of the higher socioeconomic classes[21] – but undereducated women are, in general, shut out of the professions and careers wherein one may earn a self-supporting, living wage.

In our own U.S. history, just 4 and 5 decades ago, women as a class (no matter their race or socioeconomic status[22]) – as soon as they got pregnant, (or preemptively, as soon as they got married, because it was assumed that they would shortly get pregnant, and that, repeatedly) – were routinely fired from jobs that put them in contact with the public.[23]

It was "unseemly" for a woman "in a family way" to be on such public display,[24] and employers didn't want to hire, train, or retain a category of worker who[25] was likely to get pregnant 4, 6, 10, or even 14 times across the next two decades.[26]

Thus, married female employees (and female employees of

---

[21] Or they may sell themselves, or be entrapped and sold, for "sex"

[22] Race and socioeconomic status *were* highly correlated with whether or not an unmarried woman was hired for a given kind of position in the first place, but pregnancy and/or the likelihood of pregnancy (i.e. marriage) were the rationale behind the routine firing.

[23] i.e. receptionist, cashier, bank teller, airline stewardess, etc.

[24] She had better be married, as single motherhood made a social outcast, and therefore, she was presumed to have a husband to "take care of her."

[25] In a heterosexual relationship and without reliable birth control

[26] With the attendant childcare issues that would entail

reproductive age) were a bad bet for business.[27]

Even when single, women as a class were denied access to entire fields, because it was presumed most female employees would marry[28] and turn up pregnant at some time.

The newspaper "Want Ads," and the job market itself, were segregated – by sex.

As a means of further limiting their access, women, as a class, needed higher scores on college and graduate school entrance exams to be admitted to higher or post-graduate education.[29] Universities, colleges, vocational training schools, and employers in general had an excuse not to admit or hire females – because they occupied a sex caste that (it was presumed, would terminate their studies or employment early, due to intended, or unintended, pregnancy – thus effectively blocking most women's participation in professional and semi-professional careers.

The various waves of women's organized collective action[30] have played an enormous role in making change, but as part and parcel of the movements for women's liberation, the impact of First World women's access to reliable female-controlled contraception, on their path to actual equality, cannot be overestimated.

---

[27] And by menopause, they had been out of the job market so long, they were viewed as having no viable skills or experience to offer.

[28] All women were presumed to be heterosexual.

[29] Standardized tests are affected by cultural and gender bias, and remain sources of discrimination against males of color and women of all colors. See: Miller, Casey W. Feb 2013. *Admissions Criteria and Diversity in Graduate School.* APS News. http://www.aps.org/publications/apsnews/201302/backpage.cfm (https://arxiv.org/pdf/1302.3929.pdf)

[30] Women's pressure for inclusion through demonstrations and anti-discrimination lawsuits

~ ~ ~

Motherless Despair

A Narrative

With deep despair, she heard the verdict she already knew. Year by year, again and again, her doctor gave the same sentence. Pregnant. But this was the 17th time. And they were simply stretched to their limit.

Her husband couldn't stop, wouldn't stop. Sex was what she was for. Sex and childbearing. He wanted sex, day after day, no matter what condition she was in. He was interested when she was postpartum. He was interested when she was big as a house. No matter the girth of her belly, he found a way to relieve himself on her – in her – night after night.

The only things that slowed him down were the mini-epidemics. Like the time the mumps swept through the house, and 10 of the 12 children, born at the time, fell ill.

And even though his salary didn't fit the bills, he still made time to get his beer at the local pub and come home feeling ornery enough to tell her to lie down, or to swat her a good one if she objected.

So the doctor had collected her urine, and "the rabbit had died," and her drunken husband would sit in the waiting room – again - while she panted and moaned another underfed mouth into their world.

She already cooked on a whim and a prayer. A morning meal for her brood was three-day-old donuts her sister slipped out of the store-front bakery, where she was paid a minimum wage of 75 cents per hour, and the bakery's left over coffee – given even to the toddlers – and only sometimes, with a splash of milk. And lunch was peanut butter, with the tiniest schmear of jelly, and three-day-old bread - again, pinched from the same bakery's refuse pile. And dinner was a solitary pound of ground meat, mixed with flour and water, then used to wet the pile of mashed potatoes that made up the bulk of the meal. Her children called it, "Hishy Hash." And that had to stretch to feed the 18-already-in-the-world-mouths around the table: father, mother, and 16 kids. How could they become 19? And when would this end? She was already 38, but her mother didn't hit the menopause until 48. She couldn't bear children another decade, but her husband wouldn't stop! *"Maybe her father had stopped? Her mother had only had the 12. . . . Maybe her father had stopped!"*

But of one thing she was sure. She couldn't stretch her drinking-husband's factory wages by one more plate.

She already didn't know what she would say to the landlord next week, or how she would keep the lights on. She already made tallow candles, whenever there was enough rendered meat fat to make them with, and kept the lights off each night, to keep down the electric bill.

And they couldn't afford a clothes dryer or a decent washer. Her old wringer washer would have to do, and her daughters would have to keep hanging the clothes on the line, and bringing them in before a thunder storm, to fold them – damp and stiff and dingy – from their exposure to the city air.

They didn't have a vacuum. Only a broom.

But he had his nightly beer, and his nightly, inebriated, two minute shot at her.

"Thank God, he's quick!" she thought. But even that thought gave her no joy.

She had to get back, to relieve her mother, who was sitting with the youngest 5. She had slipped to the doctor's while the older ones were at school.

Soon the two oldest girls would be looking to them to help with their weddings. There was no way they could even try to *"give them away."*

She shook her head, to bring herself back to the present. *"I must think about the matter at hand,"* she worried, bringing herself up short.

Once, across the backyard fence, when the girls were in school and a storm was whipping up, she had gone to bring in the washing herself, and stopped to discuss the weather with Mrs. Pritz on the other side. Mrs. Pritz had lowered her voice and whispered about Mrs. McLaughlin down the block. She noted that her stomach had started to grow last year, and then shrunk again – too soon. Somewhere in the gossip she dropped a name. A *"Dr. McInerny,"* on the other side of the park, who might have helped Mrs. McLaughlin out.

She walked home, but despite her waiting mother, went the long way 'round, cresting the park's far side – to pass his shingle.

"Could she do it? Would she burn in Hell?"

"Hell?!?" she argued internally. *"Hell? This is already Hell*!" She was staving off hunger with potatoes and donuts. She was dodging bill collectors and robbing Peter for Paul. She was already wearing the shame of not being able to help her daughters marry. She was increasingly worried that her next child, or the one after that, might be medically-harmed – even retarded – because she was too old to be having it! She was the sexual servant of a drunken fool, who didn't care what happened to his own children – who kept on making more, against her will – when he couldn't support the ones he already had!

A week later, she went to Dr. McInerny.

He was horrified at the suggestion that he might be able to help her in her predicament. He commanded her to leave and slammed his treatment room door closed behind her. Confused, as she struggled with her coat, his nurse glanced 'round, pulled her into the receptionist's space, and pressed a note into her hand.

On it was scrawled a phone number, CH 5-0746.

With a knowing look, the nurse helped her fix her coat and nudged her toward the exit.

Her fingers shook as she lifted the kitchen receiver and spun the dial. On the other end, a husky voice asked curt questions. *"Yes. He could help."* He named his price and gave her a date, three weeks away. A date. And a location. And a price she didn't have.

Except – except for the funds she'd been spiriting away from every transaction and had refused to spend.

Each time she bought or paid for anything, she took the change (not the bills), and when no one was looking, dropped it into an empty oatmeal carton, in the back of a closet. When that got full, she hid it behind a stack of boxes in an unvisited corner of the attic.

The change was there for a rainy day. She was saving it for the day when he retired, or the day when he was struck by a trolley as he stumbled home drunk, or the day when they laid him off for time out of work for hangovers.

Or for the money to simply bury him.

Or maybe she would let him go to a Potter's Field, and use it to feed "his" children a little while longer, before they all joined him on the other side – from malnutrition or starvation – when his drunken self left them even more destitute.

She began to feed the coins into paper sleeves. Rolls of quarters and dimes and nickels. Even the pennies.

She rolled and rolled, until she had the abortionist's price.

She could not see her way clear to take all of that change to the bank and turn it into bills. That would raise suspicion, raise the notice of the gossips, maybe even find its way to her husband's ear. He might beat her for sure if he found she had hidden money in change. And *"What was it for anyway?"* he would demand, as his blows rained down.

The image shook her. Usually, she acquiesced so quickly to his demands that her children rarely saw his rage. Actually, they rarely saw him at all – with his 2nd shift factory hours and his liquid after-work dinners.

She showed up at the designated location with a tote bag filled with rolled coin.

A squeaky wooden door swung open on the hand of a man, half-shadowed in the vestibule. There was no receptionist. It was a mere apartment. The yellowed, peony wallpaper was missing strips, and the front room looked cluttered. A wooden console television rang out with the sound of a bugle playing, *Charge*, as the U.S. Calvary streamed across the screen, flag flying, riding down an encampment of unarmed Indian women and children.

The kitchen table was laid with an absorbent cloth and a metal cart stood next to it, steel tools gleaming on its top shelf.

Taking the money gruffly, he eyed the rolls and counted, before pointing toward the table and grunting, gesturing that she should remove her underpants and climb aboard.

He handed her a questionably clean towel, indicating that she should bite on it, if she felt like screaming.

Without washing his hands and without any sort of pain relief or anesthesia, he inserted a cold speculum and began to dig at her cervix.

She bit the towel, reminding herself that she did this for her living children, promising herself she would find the way never to sleep with her husband again.

This was a price she intended to pay only once.

She felt him scraping around inside her. Then she felt something sharper, something like a slip and a pierce, and she groaned into her towel.

When it was over, she took the sanitary napkin from her bag, and shaking, threaded the ends through the sanitary belt loops, replaced her underwear, and headed to the door.

She shook the whole way home, drawing stares from others on the bus – vaguely aware that they shied away from her as she shook.

At home, she tried to cook dinner that night, but turned the task over to her oldest girl, Cathy, instead.

She muttered something about not feeling well, and with difficulty, climbed the stairs to bed.

By the time he came in that night, she had begun to wretch. It was mostly dry heaves, as there had been nothing on her stomach for the week leading up to the appointment. Her nerves had been too tightly strung.

Even he left her alone – for once.

By morning, the bed was soaked with her sweat – and blood. And her daughter's hand to her brow found she was burning up.

Cathy went for Mrs. Pritz, and together, they helped her down the stairs, where a policeman and an ambulance driver helped her away.

At Philadelphia General, they admitted her to the Women's Sepsis Wing. There, row upon row of women sweated, and cried their last.

The abortionist had punctured her uterine wall and intestines. The blood was a slow hemorrhage, not postpartum flow. Septicemia had spread throughout her blood stream.

Cathy sat, holding her hand, wiping her brow, promising to care for the younger kids, swearing never to marry.

Mrs. Pritz stopped by, then turned away, ashamed of any connection between her whispered gossip and the unstoppable inevitability of her neighbor's death.

A nurse bent over the deathbed, trying to coax out a signed confession, trying to wrest the abortionist's name from her fevered brain, but she never knew it.

Her 16 children, teens to infants, were abandoned to the unmitigated mercies of their drunken progenitor – motherless.

~~~

2. SPEAKING EVANGELICAL

I have been on both sides of abortion's religiopolitical fence. I grew up Roman Catholic, with thirteen years of Catholic school and devout parents who never missed church, and while my grade school and high school religion classes (taught by nuns) are far from a Master's of Divinity in Catholic apologetics – I was, nonetheless, a good student in those classes.

And I felt a call to the priesthood (though not to the nunnery).

They wouldn't take me because, in Catholic theology, by *not having a penis*, a female-bodied person cannot *"represent"* Christ.[31]

But I still felt a vocation to the ministry – so I eventually ended up on the Protestant side of the yard, in an evangelical Pentecostal stream that had, by then, been ordaining women for about eighty years.

I was a good student there as well, so to quote someone I once interviewed, *"I speak evangelical."*[32]

Which is to say that I deeply, experientially, understand the worldview and frame of mind of many on the Religious Right, and in this case, on the Religious Right's side of the abortion issue.

Before some Anti-Abortion activists began to shoot physicians, I remember thinking that Operation Rescue was a marvelous idea.

---

[31] "The son of God became flesh, but became flesh not as sexless humanity but as a male," Giertych said; and "since a priest is supposed to serve as an image of Christ, his maleness is essential to that role." Giertych, O.P., Fr. Wojciech in Francis X. Rocca. 5Feb 2013. *Why Not Women Priests? The Papal Theologian Explains.* Catholic News Service. National Catholic Reporter. https://www.ncronline.org/news/theology/why-not-women-priests-papal-theologian-explains; *Can a Woman Be a Priest in the Catholic Church? The Reasons for the All-Male Priesthood.* http://catholicism.about.com/od/beliefsteachings/f/Women_Priests.htm
[32] Citation withheld according to the confidentiality agreement of the interview.

And I have protested in a demonstration against abortion, in a "prolife" remake of hands across America.

I believed that "life" (not just "potential" life) began (read "the unique soul of the human individual was created by God") the moment the spermatozoon penetrated the ovum, thus creating the zygote.

So, I believed abortion, every abortion, even very early abortion, was murder.

And as my church encouraged, I "voted my conscience" each election. The primary question I had for each candidate was, if elected, *"On which side of the abortion issue will you vote?"*

But then, I learned some things that I didn't know, and I came to see the issue as much more complex. I came to see that the life of the woman/girl/(potential) mother matters as well – matters at least as much as the "life" of the zygote (fertilized ovum).

And I came to understand the number of ways in which the life of the woman/girl/(potential) mother could be put at risk by an undesired or unplanned pregnancy/childbirth/18+ years of child support and childrearing.

- I learned that the majority of women who oppose abortion happen to be married, hold a traditional gender role ideology, and are in a time of life in which they can envision slipping another baby into the fold, *even if* it would be at some burden to them and their already-existing family.

- I learned that, historically here (and around the world today), the same approximate proportion of women/girls have sought abortion whether it was/is legal or illegal – and for essentially the same compelling reasons.

- I learned that some of those reasons are:

  o   that they were raped

  o   that they were underage

  o   that they were impregnated by incest (underage and raped by a family member)

  o   that they were in abusive relationships and pregnancy would further bind them to that abuser, and they would also be unable to protect the potential life from that abuser (so that any child they bore with him would grow up being abused, or at least witnessing, the emotional/physical/sexual abuse of their mother)

  o   that they were too too young to become mothers

  o   that they were too too old to become mothers/become mothers again

  o   that they already had all of the children they, or their spouse, could financially provide for

  o   that they were in a state of ill-health

  o   that they were in a state of ill-health in which pregnancy was medically found to be life-threatening

  o   that the fetus was found to be in a state of ill-health that would lead to a life of limited potential, and/or constant physical pain for the child, and constant emotional pain for the parents, and could (if the parents predeceased the child) leave the child living beyond their deaths, as a burden on their extended family and/or the state[33]

---

[33] They recognized that, if allowed to develop to term, they would not be able to protect their disabled child after their deaths – leaving it subject to institutional abuse.

o that the timing of the pregnancy would derail important life plans (including plans that would economically prepare the woman/couple to support a child in the future) – having life-long repercussions for the woman/girl/(potential) mother – and thereby, for the (potential) child

o that they were in a place where great social shame would be attached to their being pregnant

o that they were emotionally not well-suited to (or emotionally-stable-enough for) parenting

o that they were financially unable to provide for – maybe even to feed or house – the potential child

o and that (assuming the sex had been consensual) – their contraception had failed

- I learned that women/girls who found it imperative to seek an abortion, but who were forced to seek one illegally, faced frighteningly unsanitary and unanesthetized procedures, often at the hands of untrained and unskilled providers[34]

    o or unintentionally harmed themselves trying to self-abort

    o and thus, **routinely died in large numbers** from **entirely preventable** complications (hemorrhage, visceral injuries, uterine perforations, bladder perforations, bowel perforations, sepsis, septicemia, septic shock. . . .).

---

[34] "The World Health Organization [WHO] defines unsafe abortion as a procedure for terminating a pregnancy that is performed by an individual lacking the necessary skills, or in an environment that does not conform to minimal medical standards, or both." and "Highly restrictive abortion laws are not associated with lower abortion rates." OBOS. 23 Mar 2014. *The Impact of Illegal Abortion*. http://www.ourbodiesourselves.org/health-info/impact-of-illegal-abortion/

- I learned that many of the women and girls who died from botched illegal abortions were already mothers, often of many many children, and desperate because their family finances were stretched beyond the breaking point.

  o Their abortion was meant to help the children they already had.

  o Their untimely death left their already-born offspring orphaned.

- I learned that <u>no one liked</u> abortion – that *pro-choice* people were not actually *pro-abortion*.

  o I came to recognize that pro-choice people preferred that people use contraception and that people's contraception not fail.

  o That pro-choice people simply faced the complexity differently than anti-choice people, realizing that there is more to the picture than the single theological question of the soul-status of the fertilized ovum (zygote → blastomer → morula → blastocyst) or early embryo.

  o That pro-choice people placed a different value on the life and outcomes of the impregnated female.[35]

  o That there are questions of the woman's/girl's life circumstances – and of the life chances of the (potential) child – whose needs do not end with a crib and a few packs of diapers, but extend outward (even if healthy and able to someday be self-supporting) for a minimum of a full 18 years of economic, physical, intellectual, and emotional support.

---

[35] In this case, the reproductively-able person with ovaries/ovum/fallopian tubes/uterus, etc. . . .

o   That pro-choice people believe children need to be born wanted – and to mothers and families prepared to care for them.

o   And that pro-choice people believe that women/girls (even after a contraceptive accident) have the (civil and moral) right of self-determination – to decide for themselves whether, *or not*, they are ready to host a developing fetus for approximately 9 physically-trying months, and to then go through the varied experience and/or trials of childbirth and delivery.

o   And that pro-choice people believe that women/girls have (even after a contraceptive accident) the (civil and moral) right of self-determination – to decide for themselves whether, *or not*, they are ready to dedicate the next 18 (or more) years to the well-being (and the good start in life) of another human being.

- I learned that the circumstances, life, and health of the pregnant woman/girl/(potential) mother matter too – and that they are not to be dismissed and demeaned as deserving of the "trouble" they have found themselves in – that women/girls who find themselves with an unwanted pregnancy were not simply negligent, or "promiscuous," or "sluts."

- I learned that no mentally-cognizant woman/girl/(potential) mother would *intentionally* use the expense and aggravation of abortion as their *preferred* (or first choice) means of contraception.

- I learned that many of those who oppose abortion, incongruously, oppose contraception as well. (*Why*????????????[36])

---

[36] The only possible reason to oppose contraception – if you also oppose abortion – is out of a worldview (or cultural/religious belief) that desires women be returned to the home, under the control of fathers and then husbands. No one who believes that women should

I realized that, when I was protesting abortion, I was one of those women –
married, in an appropriate reproductive time of life, and sufficiently classed
and supported that I could (while it would have been tough) imagine
slipping another child into the nest without catastrophically-overburdening
the family I already had). As an opponent of abortion, I was a physically
healthy, young, married, stay-at-home mother of two healthy children – on
a tight budget, yes – but with a husband paying the bills. And I could
imagine fitting a third child into our household – knowing we would be
able to care for, love, and even diaper and feed it. I was, *then*, still prepared
to dedicate 18 more years to the good start in life of another human being.
(Many of those years would have overlapped with years I was already
dedicating to the underage children already in my care.)

But then I remembered.

I had also been the teenage girl, and the young unmarried single
woman, with a pregnancy scare, in an era when abortion was illegal, with no
backup resources or social support network to absorb an unplanned child,
for whom I had no viable means of support.

I was lucky.

I didn't get pregnant in those years.

I had also become the non-traditional student in mid-life, returning to
school, leaving a marriage, and beginning a second career, for whom an
unplanned pregnancy would have been a source of economic and life-
course devastation.

I was lucky then, too. I did not get pregnant at that time, either.

So while I had been fortunate enough to have my reproductive scares
be just that – scares – I came to realize that if my scares had become

---

lead *"authentic and freely chosen lives"* (Jean Kilbourne 2010, 2000) would rationally want the
only choice for females to be between celibacy or sexual abstinence and repetitive pregnancy.

actualities (as a teen, or as the mother of nearly-grown teens), it would have meant utter shipwreck – and *I* might have sought an abortion myself.

The fact is, human sexuality and human reproduction are messy. They don't lend themselves to neat, or rigid, answers.

I had to face my own life's experience, and *the history of* women's contraceptive access, even across my own lifespan.

- **As my mother's daughter –**
    - o (as the oldest daughter of a woman who gave birth to 12 times, to 13 full-term children, in 15 years time –10 of whom were conceived before the birth control pill was legal across the U.S. for use by married women[37] – I remembered the day, quoted above, when my mother said, *"All thirteen of you were "Rhythm babies."*[38])
- That day she added, *"When the Pope gets pregnant, I'll have another one!"*
    - o And she kept her word. She went on birth control. She did not have another one.
    - o But the doctrine of the Church set her up. Forty-two years later, as she approached death, she agonized that she had *"kept God from bringing 4 to 6 more souls into the earth through her"*
        - ▪ she stopped bearing 6 years before her medically-necessary hysterectomy

---

[37] U.S. Supreme Court Griswold v. Connecticut, 381 U.S.479 (1965)

[38] The "Rhythm Method" (a.k.a. "Natural" Planning) is a Roman Catholic Church proposal for periodic sexual abstinence in which young married couples are expected to refrain from **all** sexual intercourse (and thus, all sexual interaction, as neither oral nor anal sex *nor withdrawal* [coitus interruptus – *see note 42 for the Sin of Onan, or Onanism*] are approved by the Church hierarchy) during the approximate 8 days of a woman's cycle during which she ovulates, or may have just ovulated, or is just about to ovulate. The Catholic Church also frowns on sexual intercourse during a woman's menstrual cycle. Thus the "Rhythm Method" leaves the couple only a handful of days after the end of a woman's period [*and considers her "unclean" after childbirth for 40 days for a male child and 80 days for a female child - Leviticus 12:1-5*] and another handful before the expected onset of her next period during which they may have sex without conceiving. Oh, and the Catholic Church forbids "all artificial means" of contraception – so no condoms, no IUDs, no hormonal methods, no spermicide, etc. are permitted either. Abstinence, for a little better than 2/3rds of the monthly cycle, is the ONLY permissible way to try to prevent conception. The rest is up to God. *Try that for the decades of your twenties, thirties, and forties, with a partner you are hot for . . . . and fail at that, and be fertile, and you can have 13 children like my parents. . . .*

- o And she died feeling guilty that she had not borne, and reared, 17 to 19, instead of a mere 13 children![39]

- **As my sisters' sister –**
    - o who watched her teenage belly grow, as she studied week-by-week the gestational progress of her zygote → to embryo → to fetus → to neonate)
    - o who saw her tears when the teenage father deserted her
    - o who wept as our culturally-shamed parents forced her into giving up her *much-loved, much-wanted* daughter
    - o who watched her cry – *across the years* – whenever that child was mentioned – *even after she'd had others*
- As my sister's sister, I know that adoption is not a quick and easy answer to unprepared pregnancy.
    - o I know that human offspring, brought to (or near) term, cannot generally be given away "to a good home" (*like a kitten or a puppy*) – so that the woman/girl/(potential) mother simply gets on with her life and doesn't look back.
    - o Instead, having felt their fetus move inside them, and likely having seen (*or even held*) their newborn at birth, most worry and wonder – across their lifetime – about the fate of their child, and agonize about whether or not they made the right decision. (*Are they loved? Provided for? Well-treated? Encouraged? Happy?*)
    - o I recognized – being forced – *by circumstances or authorities (including one's own parents, the grandparents)* – to give up a child you carried to viability[40] is often a devastating, life-altering, self-concept-defining, experience.

- As my friends' friend –

---

[39] One of her 13 died of SIDS (Sudden Infant Death Syndrome) at 10 weeks old.

[40] If set at the point when most newborns would be able to live on their own outside the womb *without medical assistance*, fetal viability would be set at about the 8th month. Today, fetal viability is set at the gestational weeks in which a fetus can be reasonably expected to survive – outside the womb – *with the help* of *intensive* medical intervention – 26 weeks (sometimes 23-24 weeks, but with less chance of survival and less chance of surviving without damage).

- As my congregants' pastor –

- As my clients' counselor –
  - I have watched single mothers of one (or more) pre-adolescent children – carrying *the lion's share of the caregiving* AND *the financial burden* – scrubbing floors/serving drinks/doing hair and facials/working night shift to house and feed the child(ren) they already have – when a new man, who promised them the sun, just didn't happen to have a condom whenever the moment for intimacy arrived (or once begun, outright refused to wear one or pulled it off mid-coitus without permission) [#stealthing=rape][41]
- And women in longer-term relationships, who relied on their boyfriends' good-faith[42] *coitus interruptus* (withdrawal)[43] – left

---

[41] And, often, the woman, being Christian, did not believe in having sex outside of marriage [despite her "falling" into the "sin" of it] and so, was herself unprepared (was not on hormonal birth control or an I.U.D., and did not have condoms at the ready) – but, also, didn't believe in abortion.

[42] If, at any given time, you are not amenable to a pregnancy, **do NOT make withdrawal your primary method of birth control. Withdrawal is NOT a reliable means of birth control**. It is better than nothing, but being able to get right to the moments before climax, and being able to stop the human interaction that feels that so good, at just that moment, requires near Superman-like abilities. Men do this every day, and have for all of human history, but because it is a very specific skill (*judging one's own level of arousal, without losing that arousal, while still continuing toward climax*), AND requires real determination (or true fear of making that woman, pregnant, at that time). **Withdrawal leads to many contraceptive accidents.**; "Although withdrawal has no known side effects, **interruption of the sexual response cycle** can greatly diminish the pleasure of a couple. . . . This method is estimated to have **a 27% failure rate annually among typical users**. That means that every year, over **1 in 4 people using withdrawal as their only method of birth control will get pregnant**. Failure rates will be lower for couples using withdrawal in combination with another method. Perfect users can expect a failure rate as low as 4%, which actually compares favorably to many other methods. . . . **Withdrawal has a 31% annual failure rate for teens, because they typically have less practice using this method effectively.** . . . . **Withdrawal does not offer complete protection from STDs. Lubricating fluids escape long before ejaculation** . . . [and] they . . . can transmit diseases like the AIDS virus." (Contracept.Org. [accessed 24 Aug 2016. *Ineffective Contraception: Withdrawal.* http://www.contracept.org/withdrawal.php – *bolding mine*).; "Using the withdrawal method for birth control **requires self-control**. Even then, the withdrawal method is **NOT an especially effective form of birth control. Sperm may enter the vagina if withdrawal isn't properly timed or if pre-ejaculation fluid contains sperm. The withdrawal method doesn't offer protection from sexually transmitted infections.**" Mayo Clinic.

with another mouth to feed – a redoubled daycare bill – twice the expenses – half the sleep – triple the fear of failing . . . .

- I remembered the scares and burdens – we – as women – are subject to:

  o the circumventions we make,

  o the determination and heart that sustains us,

  o and the luck – and social structures – that fail us.

[accessed] 24 Aug 2016. Withdrawal Method (Coitus Interruptus). (http://www.mayoclinic.org/tests-procedures/withdrawal-method/basics/definition/prc-20020661 – emphasis mine).; See also, Withdrawal (Pull Out Method) Video. https://www.plannedparenthood.org/learn/birth-control/withdrawal-pull-out-method
[43] The Roman church does not approve of coitus interruptus (Withdrawal). In Humanae Vitae, Pope Paul the VI wrote: "the direct interruption of the generative process [intercourse] already begun . . . [withdrawal is] to be absolutely excluded as a lawful means of regulating the number of children . . . [as] is any action which either before, at the moment of, or after sexual intercourse, is specifically intended to prevent procreation. . . ." Part of the reason for this prohibition of withdrawal may have been that, "since the role of the ovum was not learned until the nineteenth century [with the common use of the microscope], the sperm were thought to be little homunculi, miniature people, and for this reason male masturbation was sometimes called **homicide**" [!!!] [*bolding mine*] http://www.religiousconsultation.org/News_Tracker/moderate_RC_position_on_contrace ption_abortion.htm.; They also justify this position through the misuse of the Biblical story of **Onan** (Genesis 38:8–10), who was commanded by Jewish law to raise up a son to continue his deceased brother's name – via his widowed sister-in-law. He had no right to withdraw (as he did) during intercourse with her, since the sole purpose of his intercourse with her was meant to be fulfillment of a duty to his dead brother. God is reputed to have struck him dead, exacting greater retribution than called for by the Law of Moses (where "the penalty for not giving your brother's widow children was public humiliation, not death" - Deuteronomy 25:7-10). Since they "waste" sperm (homunculi), both withdrawal and masturbation have been labeled **"Onanism"** and frowned upon by the Roman Catholic church.; Now that we have ovulation kits (that the women of prior generations did not), "Natural family planning . . . requires tracking a woman's cycle and remaining abstinent on her most fertile days" Kempner, Martha. 21 Jan 2015. Pope Francis' Remarks About birth Control 'Methods' Offend Pro-Choice Catholics. Rewire. https://rewire.news/article/2015/01/21/pope-francis-remarks-birth-control-methods-offend-pro-choice-catholics/

~~~

Driving Stoned

A Narrative

I sighed as my eyes took in my son's tousled hair. Tangled in bed sheets, he pretended sleep. He had a lazy streak I blamed on his father, and a stubborn streak he came by honest, from me; but he pulled at the strings of my heart like nothing else on earth.

The divorce has not been drawn out, but it had been brutal. It had cost me nearly everything — my friends, my home church, much of my sense of self, and most of my sense of safety in the world. It had cost me everything — but this 10 year-old refusing to get up for school. And all the joy he brought me was paired with the tremendous burden of raising him alone.

His father was an elder of the church.

Without doing much, my ex-husband had risen into its inner circle.

We had grown up there, together. Two kids in the same children's church. We had known each other for all living memory — certainly, since we were both toddlers snotting up the nursery. Before we were conceived, his parents and my parents had been covenanted.

We had begun to "date," secretly, in middle school, and openly, by high school.

Our wedding had been simple, but expected. There had been a white gown, blue corn flowers, the church choir singing as I ascended the aisle on my father's arm, the appropriate smattering of bridesmaids and groomsmen, and a reception in the church hall for which the parish Women's Auxiliary had done all the cooking. On top of the homemade wedding cake, the little plastic bride and groom had been placed facing a larger, plastic, cross. The message was clear. *"Serve God first. Your marriage is subject to Him. YOU are subject to Him."*

In his wedding homily, the pastor belabored the text, *"Wives, submit yourselves unto your own husbands, as unto the Lord,"*[44] as he sped right past, *"Husbands, love your wives, even as Christ also loved the Church, and gave himself for it."*[45] And afterward, in the parish hall, I had been introduced as the new "Mrs. *Him.*" Microphone in hand, Pastor Kendall had said, *"And now, for the first time anywhere, the new Mr. and Mrs. Josiah Stevenson"* — and with that, my identity had been properly subsumed into my husband's, so that *"the two"* had become *"one"*[46] — *Josiah* . . . .

Despite our youth — our non-denominational denomination (a collectivity of independent Bible fellowships, and the fundamentalist stream from which they had arisen) didn't believe in birth control — so, married in June, I was pregnant by fall, and due that next July.

Josiah, only 18, worked in building construction with his uncle, but they fell out shortly after we returned from our "honeymoon" (backpacking in the Adirondacks), and while church doctrine preferred I only work at homemaking — before my stomach began to show, I found a handful of nonbelievers willing to pay me to make their homes sparkle, and began to pay the bills — myself — on our efficiency apartment.

I labored in their homes, until I went into labor.

As I bent over a client's toilet bowl, brush in hand, my water broke all over her newly-pristine tiled bathroom floor. I shoved her monogrammed towel up my skirt, mopped up my amniotic fluid, and drove myself to the hospital, while the homeowner called Josiah.

Jeremiah was born, loud and lusty, 30 hours later, and — as the bills grew on the desktop at home, two weeks postpartum, I

---

[44] Ephesians 5:22
[45] Ephesians 5:25
[46] Genesis 2:24: Matthew 19:6; Mark 10:8; Ephesians 5:31

strapped Jeremiah to my back, and returned to clean that client's bathroom again.

It took 18 months past his fight with his uncle, for Josiah to find paid work. But three months after that, Pastor Kendall thought he should be the youngest man to join the church board of elders, and by our third wedding anniversary, Esther (another lifelong children's church "friend") thought "my man" would look better on "her arm" than on mine.

As an elder, Josiah had gained us reserved seats in the sanctuary.

Every Sunday morning, Sunday night, and Wednesday night, he coaxed our clunker toward the church, and we arrived in our freshly-pressed "go-to-meeting" clothes. I rushed Jeremiah back to the newborn nursery, then joined Josiah in our new seats of honor.

At first it was subtle. I noticed his eyes wandering. As the women of the church found their seats, his eyes found their "*seats*" also.

But his eyes lingered longer on Esther – and I found myself aware of the 10 pounds of baby weight I couldn't get off and the heaviness of my still-nursing chest. At first, I noticed her fixing her dress in such a way as to expose a length of calf. But within a Sunday or two, his eyes were fixed as she exposed most of her thigh and "*unknowingly*" left her skirt hiked through the pastor's taking of the weekly offering.

Still, I thought Josiah a godly man, and when I increasingly awoke at night, heart pounding in a cold sweat, from dreams in which I'd come home from cleaning to find him penetrating Esther in our marital bed, I consoled myself with thoughts of his godliness. Now that he was working again, I sensed my family's resentment at all their unpaid childcare and, as I scrubbed other women's houses, I dreamt about staying home with Jeremiah – and even – about more children.

So, despite the nightly warfare with my intuition, I was still genuinely surprised that Sunday morning when the pastor called Josiah and I, and Esther, to the pulpit, to publicly rebuke *"us"* for *"our"* sin.

I remember that scene almost as if I were looking down from above.

There we were, two young women and one young man, all three of us less than 21-years-old, publicly exposed – *"for our own good"* – before the congregation.

Josiah and Esther had been discovered in the sexton's storeroom, in full-on intercourse, precariously perched on an industrial-sized mop bucket.

I was being blamed as well.

The story went that, *"If I were a proper wife"* – properly *"submissive,"* properly *"servicing"* him, properly dropping the baby-weight – *"my husband would not have strayed."*

Esther played the role of *Jezebel*.

Josiah played the role of the underserved man *"with needs,"* and thus, *"a good man who had been tempted"* – by *"female flesh"* and of *"the devil"* – *"beyond what he could bear."*

Josiah and Esther broke down, tears streaming, confessing their sin. The other "elders of the church" forgave them.

In the haze of dissociation, I did not repent.

My memory is that the church came to agree that they were the more proper couple. *"Perhaps Josiah's marriage to me had been hasty and premature,"* the elders speculated, enacted *"too young,"* and he and Esther *"would stand the test of time."* Perhaps, *"under the circumstances,"* *"their"* union was the *"actual"* will of God, or *"the will of God now"* – if not *"God's Plan A,"* then at least, *"God's Plan B."*

Josiah moved into Esther's parents' rental unit.

I left the church, and my shamed parents grumbled forward through their unpaid childcare.

Our no-fault divorce was uncontested. There was no property to divide.

Family court determined that, given his low income, Josiah's responsibility toward Jeremiah was $200 a month – $50 a week in support. I was entitled to no alimony. The marriage had been *"too short."*

He had rights to visitation, but for Esther's sake, he chose not to exercise them.

Esther – from their Jamaican honeymoon onward – played housewife, staying home while Josiah worked and, soon enough, they replaced Jeremiah with 4 half-siblings.

Jeremiah and I, and my parents, went on, without him.

Jeremiah was ten-years-old – when Stephen walked into the convenience store where I had picked up 20 hours.

He was tall and good-looking in his button-down shirt. Though he never darkened the door of a gym, he hunted and fished, and his natural bicep development made it look like he pumped iron.

He returned, day after day, to persuade me to go out with him.

I let him know that I was *"a Christian,"* and I was *"waiting for the man that God would send me."*

For a few weeks, I resisted – till he realized we had sons the same age. *"We should give them the opportunity to go fishing together,"* he said. *"Not a date,"* he insisted. *"Just two friends giving their sons the chance to make friends."* His son was *"a quiet kind of kid who could use another friend."*

He seemed safe enough.

So before dawn on the first Saturday that I could get off, a sleepy Jeremiah and I met Stephen and his son, Alex, and trooped off to the lake. He brought all the gear, and sunrise lapping on the water, enveloped in morning mists, was breathtaking and grounding. Our lovely day flowed into a lovely afternoon, and it just seemed normal to take the day's catch back to my place, for a home-caught dinner.

Stephen even cooked well – and after, he insisted he help clean up.

He regaled me with tall tales of fish he'd caught and small game that got away, while the boys – exhausted from rising early and from their hours in the sun – fell asleep together on the living room floor – TV droning hypnotically in the background.

I lit a candle, and watched the way his eyes glimmered. It seemed so natural to curl up next to him on the couch. He murmured something about disturbing his son to take him home, but I just didn't want him to go. It had been so long since I'd felt the warmth, or the strength, of a man's arms. I pulled him in for a kiss. When he murmured the words, *"Just friends,"* I pulled him in tighter.

In the haze of his lips, I had the passing realization that every month, about the same time, I missed having a husband in a deep and aching way. It had been eight long years, and as a Believer, I didn't have sex out of wedlock. Yet, about once a month I was so driven, I masturbated and told God later that I was sorry. I didn't go to the bars, and I didn't go online. I worked and took care of my son and did my best to make my meager dollars stretch to meet his needs. Eight years, eight long years, I had pushed my own needs away.

I melted into Stephen, and nearly led him to the bedroom, leaving the boys snoring side-by-side. Quietly, I locked the door behind us, and we moved into the rhythms of mating. I lost myself in the sight and scent and sense of a male body undulating with my own. My climax was a long-pent-up release, a reservoir bursting its spillway, magma erupting under high pressure.

Immediately, I was flooded with remorse.

I had offended God! I had had sex outside of marriage – the same sin that Josiah had committed against me – a sin I believed I would have to answer for, far worse than my monthly masturbation.

As an unwed, and therefore celibate, Christian, I did not own a single condom. And I had had no need for contraceptives. . . . And after my speech about being *"just friends,"* Stephen had not come prepared.

I began to sob in his arms. I began to pray, out loud, as I wept.

Stephen was startled. *Had he hurt me? Had he misread my signals? Had he had my consent?*

I assured him that it was *"not his fault."* I had led him to the bedroom. *I* had locked the door. *I* had been all over him. It had been consensual – in the instinctual part of my brain. But I had violated the cognitive, committed, conscious part. I had broken my own moral code.

He held me tightly and let me weep. And as he did, I sought his mouth again, for comfort. And he kissed me tightly, to reassure me, murmuring that, *"God would surely understand – that God couldn't condemn anyone as beautiful as me."*

And we made love again. And we climaxed again, sharing bodily fluids again, still without a barrier.

Three weeks later, my period still hadn't arrived. Whenever Stephen came into the convenience store, I hurried to the back on some pretended business or another.

Increasingly, my stomach got touchy and my breasts sore. By the fourth week, my period didn't show up either. But my belly eventually did, and Stephen called me on it – insisting he would take care of us.

I couldn't even think of an abortion. It was *"a sin."* It was *"murder."* It was *"the sin of murder."* But my job, as far as taking care of Jeremiah, had been difficult enough. *"How much more would a second child cost? How much time would be lost from work during the pregnancy? While I was post-partum? How would I stay ahead of the bills? My mother was gone. Who would babysit this time?"*

The pressures of the pregnancy just seemed unbearable.

Stephen offered financial help that somehow stopped after the abortion-on-demand window of my first trimester closed.

It turned out, in truth, he was downright stingy. When we ordered take-out, he'd rifle through my purse for bills and loose change and take whatever he could find. More often than not, I paid for most everything.

We tried to spend time, to see where that would take us.

I found we had next to nothing in common. Fishing and hunting were his sole passions. He didn't like my taste in anything – music, movies, museums, restaurants, clothes. And it turned out he was a stoner. He smoked weed day and night – waking and baking. And 7 out of 7 nights, he was an angry drunk – an angry drunk who slapped his kid, just for what he called "G.P." (general principle).

And he drove drunk. And since he was never not stoned, he also drove high.

As my new man, he thought his needs and desires should trump every want or need of my own. Jeremiah came to hate him, and once or twice he tried to stand up to him, but Stephen loomed threateningly over him, barking orders to all those beneath him – Alex – and me – and my Jeremiah.

As the icing on the cake, he tried to get me to give up my current church home. He didn't like my church family. It was interracial, and that bothered him. With horror, I realized he regularly used racial epithets, freely, now that he thought he had me trapped.

When I let him know I was no longer interested in developing a romantic relationship, he let me know that I would never be free of him. He saw a lawyer and informed me of his intent to seek his full paternal rights.

The pregnancy dragged on. Somehow, the baby seemed to lie in a position that aggravated my sciatic nerve, and by my 6th month, the back discomfort was excruciating. I developed a limp and spent whatever time I wasn't on my feet cleaning houses, or making sandwiches at the store, with my feet up and a heating pad.

When my labor pains got to 4 minutes apart, I drove myself to the hospital.

I didn't call Stephen.

They checked me, but the pains didn't get any closer together, so they called them Braxton-Hicks, and sent me home again. Still, they hurt, and they were regular, and it was impossible to sleep through them. Two more days passed, before, exhausted, I called a sister in the church to drive me back. I swore her to secrecy, and again, I didn't call Stephen.

I was still at just 3 centimeters and only partially-effaced, but seeing my exhaustion, they decided to break my water. The labor intensified. After 28 more hours of labor, where I thought my back was breaking, they decided to do a Caesarean. I say they decided because, by then, I was in such an altered state of consciousness, so lost in the pain, that I could no longer respond to their questions.

Jessica was delivered at 7 pounds, 10 ounces. She was 19 inches long, with jet-black curls, and a bruised right eye and forehead – bruised from the labor. As they put her in my arms, I vowed to take care of her – forever.

It was 6 weeks before I could fully walk upright.

Less than two weeks after her birth, Stephen showed up at the front door, an emergency custody order in hand. Pending a successful paternity test, the paper said that a judge had granted him temporary visitation with the expectation of full joint custody – joint medical, joint legal, and shared residential.

Starting as soon as the swab was tested, it would establish his right to visit with her alone and unsupervised, to – even while I was nursing – take her between feedings and begin to establish his relationship with her. He had the right to take her, bring her back in two hours to feed, then take her away again, three times each day – seven days a week.

I couldn't imagine where I would get the money to fight him in court.

And, of course, I knew the paternity test would establish him as the father.

When he came for his first morning's visitation, a faint scent of beer struck my nose, as he gleefully lifted her from my arms and strapped her in the car seat carrier he'd brought.

When he brought her back two hours later, her Onesie reeked of weed . . . .

~ ~ ~

3. IMPREGNATION AS ABUSE

(as Control of a Woman*/Girl*)

In my years of ministry, and in my general life experience, I have known really good fathers, really good mothers, really good well-prepared couples, and really loving families.

But also, in my years of ministry, it has become apparent that (deceitful or damaged) human beings can put their best (relationship) foot forward for quite some time, and that human libido is NOT the best judge of human character.

When people are sexually attracted, the person to whom they feel that attraction may not always be the best choice with whom to co-parent. But they rarely know that at the outset.

And sometimes, before a woman has time to fully assess a partner's character (which can take months or even years), she[47] is already pregnant.

If a man is not a good man – not a good partner – but is domineering and controlling and wants to trap a woman (and thus, violate her freedom of choice) – one form of preplanned abuse may be to complain about condoms, get her to trust his skill at withdrawal (coitus interruptus, a.k.a. "pulling out") and then, if he fears her abandonment (if he senses her emotionally pulling away and, thus, potentially escaping from his control), have one or more "inexplicable" contraceptive "accidents" – and fail (*oh so apologetically*) to pull out "in time." *Oops!!!*

---

[47] Or he, if a transman with a uterus decides to have, and carry, a child to term.

This door swings both ways. There are also controlling and insecure women in this world, and while they may play the dominance game differently, there are women who seek to trap a man by lying about being on hormonal contraception and planning to get pregnant.

Men who do not want to be trapped, or who are not ready to be fathers at this time with this woman, also need to assess the character of the woman/women in whom they are releasing sperm AND to keep themselves from releasing (or leaking) sperm intravaginally – by using the male-controlled-method of birth control – the condom[48] – until they are ready to have a planned child, with a chosen woman, whom they have ascertained, will make a good mother to their child/children.

If the woman, thus impregnated,

- has moral qualms about the morning-after pill/emergency contraception, or abortion – or

- does not have access to choice –

or if:

- the man can convince her to give him just one more chance – and spin a tale in which a baby fixes everything wrong between them –

he is in her life – and in her child's life –

- for life. . . .

You can never truly be done with someone with whom you procreate.

Whenever any woman has a baby with any man, that man is – or can

---

[48] Preferably with a sperimicidal lubricant. The combination of condom WITH spermicide bring this methods reliability up to the reliability rate of hormonal methods.

be, at his own discretion – in that child's life – for life.

There is a certain biological truth to this. And there is a definitive legal truth to it. Fathers have paternal rights, even as mothers have maternal rights.

If he is a good man, she will likely want him there – fulfilling his role as father – helping parent and provide.

If he is a bad man, whether she wants him there or not, he will damage the child(ren) that she bears – either by his absence – or by his presence.

> *The converse is also true. If a man procreates with a woman who is unfit to be a mother – he and the child(ren) he has through her – will both suffer. But, in this discussion, we are on the topic of a woman deciding – if she knows in time – whether or not to carry the embryo of an abuser to term, and so we will limit our discussion to the one side.*[49]

Even if she – *recognizing that they, as a couple, are not right for each other* – personally walks away, a man still has parental rights and can assert them through the family court system and a paternity test. And he can – if he so desires – use his rights to the child(ren) she chooses to carry to (or near) term, as a fulcrum with which to control and dominate her life.

If he is a bad man, and an unworthy father –

- He can punish her through her children (both those that are his and those that are not).

---

[49] Because it is the person-with-a-uterus who must go through the months of gestation, the labor and delivery, the post-partum recovery, and who is – generally – then, primarily, responsible for the 18 years of underage childrearing – however well or poorly done.

- Whether she stays or goes, he can manipulate the child(ren) into rejecting her most cherished values, into seeing her hard work for their financial well-being as her choosing job or career over them, into seeing any human foible she may have as something that invalidates her as a person and/or as a mother.

- He can alienate her child(ren)'s affections, telling them – if she won't be with him – what *"a "b__ch" their mommy is for breaking up their family,"* or if she stays with him, what *"a "b__ch" their mommy is for burning dinner."*[50]

- Through various forms of abuse – physical/sexual, psychological/ emotional, even *financial* – he may pressure her to distance herself from her other child(ren) – insisting she ship off ones that aren't his to their birth father(s) or extended family.

- He can punish her by (physically/verbally/emotionally and sexually) abusing her child(ren) (hers alone, and theirs jointly) – and only rarely lose his parental custody/visitation rights.

And if she firmly leaves him, he can frame any new romantic relationships she has as another way that, *"Mommy doesn't care for them, because she is just a self-centered "b__ch"* – while presenting his new woman as the perfect replacement "mom" that makes him, and his new relationship, the perfect nuclear parenting unit . . . .

---

[50] This kind of verbally putting down your child(ren)'s other parent is frowned upon by family court – but happens, daily, nonetheless, usually without repercussion.

~ ~ ~

Pulling Out

A Narrative

I caught him. He kept doing it, and I caught him – again. He had promised. Said he loved me. Sobbed like a baby. Begged me not to leave. Got down on one knee and buried his head in my lap. Reminded me of all we'd been to one another.

But I was resolute. Determined not to give in.

She was all over his social media. Facebook. Instagram. Multiple messaging apps on his phone.

I made him give me all the passwords. Couldn't catch him on SnapChat, but the evidence was overwhelming.

My intuition had been keeping me up at night. I would wake from nightmares with the smell of her stuck in my nostrils.

At work, my mind would play over and over again, the long evening hours when he'd barely grunt at me but keep slipping his cell phone out, turning its face away, then slipping it back into his pocket whenever I'd get near, telling me when the notifications went off that it was just the guys at work.

She pretty much blew up his phone, each night, all night, till he would turn the ringer off and fall asleep with it under his pillow.

Then, for a couple of weeks, everything went quiet. No notifications beeping. No pulling out the phone. No whispered calls in the bathroom. And my guts started to uncurl.

And during those weeks, he bought me flowers, twice – just because. And he'd taken me out to dinner. And he'd talked

43

about how much it meant to him, living together with me. And he'd sworn never, ever, to get emotionally invested in someone else again. He even confessed – to *emotional* cheating – but swore up and down he'd never touched her – never even met her face-to-face.

And I'd let my guard down. And we made love, seven times in those two weeks. Sweetly, softly, like we used to. And he looked deeply into my eyes while he mouthed, *I love you*, as he came.

And he withdrew, like he always did.

But once or twice, toward the end of the two weeks, he forgot. He apologized profusely. *"It just felt so good. I just felt so connected,"* he'd *"slipped up"* and didn't *"fully"* pull out in time. He meant, he *"pulled out,"* just *not "fully on time."* He was *"sorry"* if maybe it *"leaked a little"* before he *"remembered"* himself. One of the times he even moaned, *"Oh, ssshhiittt… "* and pumped another time or two, before he withdrew.

And then my period didn't come. But *"it was okay,"* I told myself, *"because he loves me."* I told myself, *"We love each other. This will work out."*

And when I told him about my period, he got really happy, and he rushed to the drug store and came back with three different pregnancy tests, *"Just to make sure,"* he said – so excited at the prospect of our making a baby together – because he *"loves me soooo much!"*

And one after the other, the strips changed color when I peed on them, and one got that little plus sign in the center.

And he talked about building me a crib by hand, in his workshop, and helping me pick out paint colors for the nursery – light green and yellow – because we would be happy no matter what sex or gender *"our"* baby was.

And I started to get happy. And to forget. I started to forget all the times he'd teetered on the edge of rage with me in the past. *"He'd stopped himself,"* I consoled myself and dismissed the memories. And I let myself forgive the way he'd responded to that Slut's texts and private messages. I let myself believe that he'd only *"been messing with her to get even with"* me, *"because old bald Kevin at work had tried to kiss me at the last company Christmas party."* I let myself believe he'd cheated emotionally – only emotionally – because his *"manhood had been challenged"* when I *"hadn't reported Kevin to higher ups,"* even though I'd told him how Kevin was the CFOs uncle and every other girl he'd messed with had been *"let go"* for spurious reasons soon after she pointed the finger.

I missed my second period, and started having to dress differently.

He never showed up the day I went to the paint store, but I came home with green and yellow anyway, and started to work on the nursery, clearing out old file boxes for floor space for the crib and prepping the walls.

Then I'd caught them. Actually caught them. In the act. In our own bedroom. In MY bed!

I'll never forget the view from the doorway. It seared itself into my neurosynapses. Her legs, pale thighs and all, lifted up onto his shoulders, hooker heels jutting out into open air. And his ass, black peach fuzz pumping into the gorge.

I froze. I literally didn't know what to do. Thought may actually have stopped. I couldn't really comprehend the scene.

Till she saw me, and she started pounding on his back. At first, he pumped all the harder, misinterpreting her signal for passion. When she screamed, he finally looked at her face, with that same expression he often wore when he looked into mine, midflight. But her horror made him glance over his shoulder.

If my heart hadn't been on that floor, the way he jumped up and off my bed might have been funny. In fact, the move he executed might have been damned near impossible, even for an Olympian, but there he was, standing, penis wet and erect, standing on our floor, only feet from her legs, spread open on my purple-flowered quilt.

My feet came unglued from the boards, and I turned, and fled down the stairs, Jeff following me, now-limp penis flopping as he ran. He caught me, screaming, *"How dare you? How dare you judge me? Slut that you are! I'll show you! I'll take you to court. I'll win my baby, and give it to her to raise. She'll be a better mother than you ever could be. I have rights! And you better not leave me 'til after you give birth. You better not leave me, or I'll prove you unfit!"*

He yelled that he'd gotten me *"pregnant on purpose,"* so he – and she – could *"raise"* my kid.

He claimed he'd *"kept detailed records"* of each time we'd done weed together, but written it down as only my transgression. And the times we'd done 'shrooms in the woods. He'd *"kept a record"* of that too. But he was never there. He wrote it down as if someone had told him, and he had had it verified. And if I did anything too funny, he'd *"dose up my food or drink, and make sure my drug tests came back dirty"* anytime he took me to court for custody.

I screeched out of the driveway, unaware – until later – of how he must have looked, standing in the end of the cul-de-sac, in front of his inherited two-story colonial, dripping her wetness onto the asphalt driveway.

Then the barrage started. Call after text after wall post, about what a "whore" I was and how I'd better come back to him. My parents' house was barraged by florists, handwritten notes enclosed, about how sorry he was, and how wrong. Petitions to, *"Please, come "home."* And promises, *"he'd never do it again."*

Marching into that abortion clinic was one of the toughest things I've ever had to do.

I wanted a child, and until just weeks before, I had very much wanted a child with him. But as I approached 10 weeks, I knew, it was now, or forever hold my peace, as he fought me across its childhood for custody. As he, across my child's childhood, alienated its affections from me. As he fought to give my child to another woman, any other woman who didn't/ wouldn't/ couldn't ever leave him.

My resolve was firm within me. I couldn't have HIS child, or ever after, he would control my life and damage the life – and mental health – of whatever I brought to term.

The staff was polite and respectful. They explained, I had to receive counseling, and then wait 24-hours, to see if I changed my mind. I didn't figure that 24-hours would do anything for *his* mind.

The procedure would not be covered by insurance, unless I could demonstrate that I had been impregnated by rape. *Did intentional failure to withdraw, in order to get me pregnant and then give my baby to another woman, constitute rape?*

I returned the second day. As the staff checked with me periodically, to see how I was doing, silent tears of relief and regret rolled down my face. I was relieved to cut the tie to him once and for all. Part of my heart was grateful beyond words that I had the choice NOT to bear his child and be bound to his abuse, and his determined Infidelity, for life. Not to have *my* child bound *to him* for life . . . .

And part of me was angry – at me – for ever having believed or forgiven him, after I'd seen his texts and posts, after I'd read their online courtship.

It's taken me a long time to forgive myself for having given him the opportunity –

recognizing that I was pulling away –

to fail to pull out.

And part of me knows that I will never understand his craziness. His character, or lack thereof, is – was – beyond my ability to compute.

I know only this. He had become involved with someone else and, rather than letting me go, he did his best to impregnate me – and it worked. And somehow he thought that, wherever he went, whomever he was with, the child would be *his* – his property – and if I caused him any problems, he would work to have me declared unfit and to take it from me.

I could not envision the hell – of being bound to the hell – of being bound – by a child – to him – for life.

~~~

4. PATERNAL RIGHTS &

THE FAMILY COURT SYSTEM

Whatever your sex[51] or gender[52] or sexual/affectional[53] orientation–
whomever you procreate with is remarkably important – and your
procreation should – as much as possible, be chosen – and *thoughtfully*
chosen.

The partner(s) you procreate with will dramatically affect your life – and
the lives of any and all children you have.

Whomever you procreate with has rights[54] – generally joint rights[55] –
throughout the 18 years of minority (childhood). A father[56] – more easily
than a mother – can (if he chooses) walk away. Biologically-speaking, it is
impossible for the pregnant woman who chooses to carry (or who has no
access to pregnancy-prevention or abortion) to "walk away" from her own

---

[51] *female, male, intersex, third, etc.*
[52] *cisgender, transgender, gender-fluid/gender nonconforming, etc.*
[53] *straight, gay, bisexual, pansexual, etc.*
[54] Actual donors, through a sperm donation clinic, excepted.
[55] And, legally, joint responsibilities – though this is highly **under**-enforceable through the family court system. It simply doesn't work out that way, in part, because of gender roles within couples, and in great measure, because of inherent inequality (based on historic sexism and misogyny) in the court systems. Historically, children "belonged" to, were solely the property of, the male progenitor (or, in the event of his death or incompetence, his nearest male heir). Women's rights to their own children, in court, are of recent origin (mid-20th Century) and are still fraught with routine prejudice and discrimination.
[56] Despite attempts to regulate through "*Deadbeat Dad*" laws

body.[57] A father also can (if he chooses) stay – whether for good or for ill.

A father who has not been involved (whether through the pregnancy, or through the years of early childrearing, or even through an entire childhood) can show back up – and have as many rights as if he'd never walked away.[58]

And while it is possible, it is both difficult and costly to prove a parent – any parent – unfit.

In a separation or divorce, many fathers are sincerely interested in responsibly co-parenting their children and – at least in front of the children – honor the woman(women) with whom they've have children.

But in our present-day culture – heir to approximately 6000 years of patriarchy – other fathers use children as trophies in a power game – a gendered tug-of-war. And while mothers can also be the villains in this game of alienation of affection[59] – **statistically – the balance of power in this contest is *not* equal.**

In part, because of the experience of carrying to term, the people with the plumbing to conceive and gestate, often end up with a more protective bond toward their child(ren). They are also faced with higher social expectations that they will indeed bond with their children – that they will "be there" – parenting, protecting, and providing – for the long haul.

So, in a discussion of conception and *contra*-ception, it is important to touch on the times in which **the maternal part of the potentially-**

---

[57] Though there certainly are abusive and/or negligent mothers.

[58] And his rights will have nothing to do with whether or not he married the mother, or whether or not either of them have (before or since) married others.

[59] Women are also subject to the full range of ways in which human beings can be trouble – or troubled.

procreating pair should consider the character of the paternal part of the potentially-procreating pair – before deciding whether or not to gestate (or carry) an unintentionally-fertilized ovum to (or near) term.

In other words, when impregnated, a woman should **think about the man's character before she chooses to carry** his seed, because **from that time forward, *his character* will affect her – and any child she bears** via his sperm – **as much as anything ever can.**

Ideally, **every child should be wanted**, even planned, **and have one or more emotionally-mature and loving parent(s)/guardian(s)** – who (each) take real responsibility – sharing the work and finances of childcare, and actively (co)parenting throughout the years of minority.

All children should have parents who do not injure or neglect, and parents who do not use their offspring as emotional footballs in adult power struggles and games of control and abuse.

We have a cultural rhetoric that claims that the Court system has the "best interests of the child" at heart. Yet, when a child is born – **no matter who does the caregiving and providing,**[60] and no matter how they treat each other – or the child – **both parents are considered** by the courts **to have "rights" to the child.**

Even today, a child is property.

This view of parental rights equivalates to a view in which the child, to

---

[60] In heterosexual, dual-parent households, this financial and caregiving work is, lopsidedly, done much more frequently and consistently by the mother.

the Court,[61] is **parental property**[62] – and (culturally) we are **only recently emerged from a long history** of child(ren) being viewed as **the *exclusive* property of the father.**[63]

And **parents who are insecure and controlling** can and do use those "rights" as a fulcrum *to assert power over* and dominate the other parent (and the child) – as they come and go from the child's life.

Generally, the courts are **NOT** actually foregrounding "the best interests of the child." Instead, their focus is to establish **equivalencies** for each parent, so that – no matter what evidence is presented – custodial conflicts are **not** generally considered to be grounded in actual paternal or maternal wrongdoing, such as neglect or abuse. Rather, **parental custody disputes are minimized and dismissed as mere "feuding."**

Parents of any sex/gender/orientation can be wonderful.

And parents of any sex/gender/orientation can be neglectful or abusive.

And despite the intensity of the bond that can develop between mother and child (through the long process of gestation, birthing, nursing, and nurturing) – men are as capable – if they will – of being as good parents (of nurturing) as women are expected to be (men can bond).

Nevertheless, in our culture, mothers still make up the majority of childhood caregivers, especially during infancy and the toddler/preschool years.

---

[61] In fairness to the courts, children are very vulnerable, and no system has been devised that can take the place of actual loving parents in the goal of keeping children safe, secure, and well-treated, that they might grow up self-supporting and able to make a contribution to society.

[62] Property for which they are supposed to be responsible.

[63] i.e. patriarchy = rule of the father

And, nevertheless, in our culture – **because** we socialize males into an ubiquitous hegemonic model of hyperviolent masculinity – and into the **dominance over**, and the **subordination of**, women and children – **statistically** – males make up the overwhelming percentage of *physically* violent and/or *sexually abusive* partners and parents.[64]

The rates of child abuse are simply epidemic in our society.

For the last few decades (and only for the last few decades), there have been laws on the books against child abuse, but courts still frequently back the **"rights"** of fathers – even when they have been **demonstrated** to be physically and/or sexually abusive to **"their"** child(ren).[65]

---

[64] Women are not morally superior. Women can have psychological issues and be emotionally-abusive and controlling, in the same range of ways as men. And women can physically attack a male or female partner (or a child). However, in part because of our gender socialization, and in part, because of differences in upper body strength that are a facet of the secondary sexual characteristics developed in male puberty, both the rates (socialization) and the physical impact (upper body strength) of male-on-female violence are widely disparate. In general, when a woman hits a male partner it may hurt, but when a man hits a female partner his hands and arms have the capacity to be lethal weapons against her. (And of course, an enraged parent, of either sex, can use their bodies as a lethal force against a child.) In a physical assault, size matters.

[65] "Sexual assaults are punished as serious felonies, often resulting in the lengthiest terms of incarceration meted out by the state. When the perpetrator is an adult and the victim is a child, many states further enhance the penalty for sexual assault by increasing the minimum available sentence and creating more stringent conditions for release. However, many states **offer a discounted criminal charge** to perpetrators of child sexual assault **who are related to their victims**. Loopholes written into state laws **permit related perpetrators who have been convicted** to escape penalties which would otherwise be mandatory for child sexual offenders, including imprisonment, mandatory sentence enhancements, and sexual offender registration. Prosecutors may offer **probation-only sentences** and forms of judicial diversion available **only to related perpetrators**. In some cases, the **convicted perpetrator** may **return to live in the home of the child-victim"** [and/or receive unsupervised **visitation/joint custody/or full custody – as the child is removed from the care of the co-victim/non-offending ("non-protective") parent – often the mother) and turned over to the probated perpetrator** (statistically, generally the father)]. Andrew, Ruby P., 24 May 2006. *Child Sexual Abuse and the State: Applying Critical Outsider Methodologies to Legislative Policymaking. Abstract* . UC Davis Law Review, Vol. 39(5). http://ssrn.com/abstract=904100; "... when fathers 'grow their own victim,' [they are generally not] held accountable like other offenders. . . . Even if police do take a report of sexual abuse perpetrated by a

Even when there is sufficient evidence, the courts are suspicious of claims by one (generally the female) parent that the other (generally the male) parent is an abuser – **viewing these claims as mere hype or rhetoric** in the separation/divorce conflict **between warring former lovers** – disbelieving the (generally female) accuser.[66]

---

family member, **chances are very good that the perpetrator,** even if convicted, **will get off lightly compared to an outside-the-family perpetrator.** . . . [T]he law in many states maintains **gaping legal loopholes** where, **prosecutors** can, and frequently do, **charge intra familial child sex abuse under different codes which allow the family offenders much lighter sentences.** In addition, **the law allows convicted intra familial child sex offenders to be given probation, different from outsider child sex offenders who must go to prison. And the law allows convicted intra familial child sex offenders to stay off the state's public registered sex offenders lists, also unlike 'outside.'** (For a good discussion of the legal loopholes for fathers and other family members who sexually molest their children see Child Sexual Abuse and the State by Ruby Andrew at http://papers.ssrn.com/sol3/papers.cfm?abstract_id=904100). There isn't a civic leader out there that doesn't publicly rage to the heavens about what monsters child molesters are, and how these 'animals' should be strung up at the crack of dawn. But . . . **the overwhelming majority of all child sex abuse is perpetrated by family members.** What this means is that, in reality, we have a system that publicly beats its chest over the small percentage of child molesters who attack someone else's child, while by legal slight of hand **that same system lets the vast majority of child molesters go free. Not by accident, but by legal and institutional design.** What's perhaps most telling is that . . . **these legal loopholes for intra familial perpetrators have been widened over recent years, rather than tightened.** Or to put it another way, the more women and children have made demands on the system to stop family violence, the more the system has created ways to look good, while paving the perpetrator's escape. The patriarchy with all its bluff and bluster to the contrary, still supports the notion that a man's home is his castle, and that **his** children **are** *his to do with as he pleases.* Unfortunately, CPS [Child Protective Services], with its *hold-no-perpetrators-accountable system,* is a vital part of the machinery for perpetuating these archaic and oppressive beliefs." JusticeWomen.com. 2010. *Beware Child Protective Services: What Victims, Advocates, and Mandated Reporters Need to Know.*
http://justicewomen.com/tips_bewarechildprotectiveservices.html (emphasis mine).
[66] "I had been trained to be suspicious of abuse claims during divorce cases. Child Protective Services said the allegation was unfounded — as a new judge I thought 'We'll just do 50-50 custody and move along. . . . I've changed my practices and tried to open my eyes," she said. "I was told not to believe people in divorce when they make claims about sexual abuse or domestic violence." Former Judge DeAnn Salcido, J.D. In MCMoewe. 25 Aug 2014. *Judge: I Gave a Child Molester Custody of His Daughter.*
http://www.dailykos.com/story/2014/8/25/1324443/-Judge-I-Gave-a-Child-Molester-Custody-of-His-Daughter; "Safe Kids International founder Cindy Dumas . . . wrote . . . "Children are being routinely placed into the custody of abusers and molesters, and mothers are being retaliated against when they try and protect their children. It is time to come together and demand these human and civil rights be enforced. . . .We've gotten the right to vote, we have the right to work but we haven't gotten the rights in the family. When we try to enforce our rights in the family in the courts it doesn't work. There is an agenda to keep

Along with ignoring or dismissing evidence, this perspective fails to take into consideration the proven emotional/psychological **harm to children** of **witnessing** abuse to, or between, parents. The courts make little to no effort to protect children from living with adult-on-adult physical/emotional/verbal/sexual violence.

Even when there has been a long history of domestic violence calls by the mother to the police, the demonstrated fact that a father has physically abused the mother of "his" child(ren), or stepchildren, is **considered to have no bearing on** his relationship with those child(ren) – except when there is an actual criminal conviction for domestic violence – and even then, he is likely to be *entitled* to unsupervised visitation with the children, and may go through a process to gain back his full custodial **rights.**[67]

Further, even when a father has been demonstrated to have physically abused (not just his adult partner but also) "his" child(ren),[68] the courts

the fathers in control." Cindy Dumas, J.D. In MCMoewe. 25 Aug 2014. *Judge: I Gave a Child Molester Custody of His Daughter.* http://www.dailykos.com/story/2014/8/25/1324443/-Judge-I-Gave-a-Child-Molester-Custody-of-His-Daughter.

[67] "IF, in the last 5 years: a parent w[ere] convicted of domestic violence against the other parent OR any court has decided that 1 parent committed domestic violence against the other parent or the children," THEN, "the judge will treat your case as a domestic violence case," and "usually, when a judge decides that your case is a domestic violence case, the judge cannot give custody (joint or sole custody) to the parent who committed domestic violence. BUT [even then] that parent can get parenting time with the children ([unsupervised] visitation rights)" – AND "a judge CAN [restore] joint **or sole** custody to the parent who committed domestic violence if the parent who was abusive: proves to the court that giving joint or sole custody of the children to him or her is in the best interest of the children; has successfully completed a 52-week batterer intervention program; has successfully completed substance abuse counseling if the court ordered it; has successfully completed a parenting class if the court ordered it; is on probation or parole and has complied with the terms of probation or parole; **has a restraining order** against him or her and has followed the orders; and has not committed any further domestic violence." California Courts. [accessed] 24 Aug 2016. *Children and Domestic Violence.* http://www.courts.ca.gov/1268.htm

[68] "[N]o matter how serious the abuse, it is highly unlikely the courts will completely sever

(working from that idea that child(ren) are property to be divided between contesting parties),[69] also hold the idea that **child(ren) NEED** *interaction* **with** – *rather than protection from* – abusive fathers (and sometimes, mothers).

Therefore, the **courts routinely seek to reinstate the custody/ visitation of proven abusers** – with only a minimal show of obedience to mandated counseling sessions or anger management classes.[70]

As already demonstrated in the footnotes for this chapter, this may remain true, even when the parent is a sexual offender – and has offended against his own (and/or his partner's other) child(ren).[71]

---

the relationship between the children and their father. What the courts will very likely do is supervise the relationship between the children and their father. . . ." Woman's Justice Center. 2010. *The Greatest Escape: Special for Victims of Domestic Violence.* http://justicewomen.com/tips_escape.html

[69] Wright Glenn, Amy. 28 Jun 2015. *Ordered to Live With An Abuser: How and Why American Family Courts Fail Children.* PhillyVoice.com. http://www.phillyvoice.com/live-abuser-american-family-courts-fail-children/

[70] ibid; Note: psychological services can be of great help to the motivated individual looking to heal, but short-term and /or court-mandated programs are unlikely to have any lasting effect, one, because real change generally takes years and because the errant parent is insufficiently motived, as shown by the fact that they had to be court-mandated. Therapy was not sought on their own, or for the sake of their child(ren). It is complied with, in the short-term, so their "property" may be returned to them (and in order not to be found in contempt of the court).

[71] Arlaine Rockey, J.D., Arlaine. 2003. *Custody Cases: Protecting Children From Child Abuse.* https://protectingourchildrenfrombeingsold.wordpress.com/about/custody-cases-protecting-children-from-sexual-abuse/

~ ~ ~

Witness for the State

A Narrative

He was exactly the rapist we are taught to fear. While most rapes are committed by perpetrators we know – and often – trust, this was the actual stranger rapist, the one who shows up only 22% of the time – the guy with the knife or the gun, and the elements of the dark and of surprise.

I was walking home from the bar. That *"didn't help my case,"* the beer-bellied mustachioed cop muttered, as he took down *"the facts."* Never mind that I was wearing sweats and a giant overcoat, and that my hair was pulled back in a ponytail at the nape of my neck and covered in a baseball cap, and that I was makeup-less.

I had stopped on my way home from babysitting at my mother's for an 11pm beer at a local pub. And I was young and thin and, at least in the old fat cop's estimation, *"not ugly,"* and when uncovered, my hair was *"bleach-blonde."* In his police report, I was a *"loose woman"* on the street at midnight, having *"consumed some alcohol."* Perhaps the assailant had *"mistaken me for a streetwalker,"* since I was walking the street at night. Perhaps he had thought that I was *"for sale,"* even though his only payment was the knife blade against my neck. Perhaps he had seen me, without the overcoat, in the pub, and followed me out, thinking I was *"asking for it."* *"Some guys are like that,"* the cop said. They think, *"with the way you look,"* that *"you want them."* Then, *"they get punished for misreading your intentions."*

The physician between my legs finished combing my pubic hair for the assailant's public hairs, and secured his combings next to the fluids he had already collected from my vagina – while the male cops stood too far south of the medical sheet covering my thighs, where they could, between their jottings on the police forms, sneak a furtive peek – or a prolonged ogle – at my exposed vulva.

The female nurse seemed oblivious to all the men around my lower half, and I closed my eyes to blot them out.

Then, I was pretty much stripped the rest of the way, as the police photographer posed me, angle by angle, to document all of my wounds and bruises.

And the physician, stitching the places I'd been merely sliced, noted, *"You were lucky, Young Lady,"* pointing out *"the proximity"* of some of my wounds *"to vital organs."*

Lucky. . . .

Despite the unfavorable police report, the D.A. decided to prosecute. There had been a series of "incidents" in that section of Fort Wayne, and the DNA matched some of the other, recent, rape kits; and he thought, with my testimony, he had a case.

Later that week, they brought me in for the lineup. It didn't matter that I wanted nothing to do with it.

My roommates had taken me to the hospital. I hadn't wanted to go, but they had insisted when I wouldn't stop bleeding, and thus, this whole second nightmare had begun.

From behind, and then, in the dark, on top of me, I had not gotten a full look at my assailant, but the one I picked out of the lineup (based more on the tenor of his voice than his visage), turned out to match the DNA from the pubic hair and sperm.

And since he matched for the other women, too, we were all informed we would be subpoenaed to testify. We must show up, or they would arrest us for contempt of court. We were, not plaintiffs, but "witnesses for the state."

The days crawled by, inching their way toward the court date. I slept as much of the time as I could, pulling the blanket over my eyes at each encroaching sunrise.

Each awakening brought it back, along with a new round of nausea, and the desire to sink back into the blessed unawareness of sleep. Unawareness, except for when I startled awake from the nightmare of the knife blade pressed against my neck, or of the delight in his voice as he etched its steel tip into my flesh or plunged it near one of those "vital organs," or of the slurping sounds he made as he climaxed his dirt into my vagina-turned-gaping-wound.

It took a good month before it dawned on me that I hadn't seen my period, maybe a month and a half to question the source of my nausea – which by now, filled my mouth at every thought of food.

My worst fears were confirmed.

My roommates thought it *"might be best"* if I *"went home"* to my mom. I hadn't worked since *"the incident,"* or contributed to the rent. They *"couldn't afford"* to spot me month after month, and *"needed"* to get another roommate to fill my place. It was hard to rent my room with me *"passed out"* in the bed, or retching over the side of it into a trashcan. I was, after all, *"stinking up the place."*

We discussed abortion. They said, between them, they could come up with, maybe, a hundred. Would my mom make up the rest?

They poured me into one roommate's car, the one owned by the only one of us with a "real job," and poured me back out, into my mother's house – most of my belongings folded neatly into one, oversized, laundry basket.

As I crawled into her bed, they told her my condition.

My mother was adamant. Her answer was, "No. Absolutely no!"

I was already 7, maybe 8, weeks along, and she was a Christian. Her church had opened "a ministry" to young mothers. They would help with a crib, a stroller, some newborn clothes and earth-friendly cloth diapers, and a set of sterilizable baby bottles. I could live with her, and while helping with her babysitting service, I could care for my own. She put her foot down. There would be no abortion for me – not in her house – not with any of her money.

I couldn't think. I pressed myself into her extra room, made a mat on the floor behind her sewing machine, and slept away another month.

By the time the court date came, I was big as a house. My mother couldn't figure out why I was showing so much, so early, but she found an old maternity top at a local thrift, repaired it on her machine, and dressed me for court.

The trial was a blur. His presence in the room kept me dissociated.

There was a judge. There were lawyers. There were his other known victims – with similar stories.

Questions flew at me. I repeated the facts that had burned into my brain, on continuous-nightmare-repeat, across the long months. His was the voice, the fear, the knife blade that glinted in my sleep-paralysis – his – the low threatening timber, "Do what I say, or tonight you die."

In retrospect, it wasn't possible. Still it never even occurred to me to try to hide my belly from him – or from the court. When they let me leave the stand, I left the courthouse. My mother told me, later – they convicted him.

I had no prenatal care. Nineteen years old, sleeping on my mother's floor, there was no insurance. So, no prenatal care. And no trauma-sensitive treatment for my mind or heart.

My mother rearranged her sewing room, and got me a used twin mattress on a steel frame. It was the best she could do. The church, she assured me, would "get us a crib – soon."

My pregnant belly and back were grateful for the real mattress.

When my labor started, my mother drove me to the E.R., where they admitted me to Maternity. She held my hand as the pain washed over me in waves. The doctor was concerned. I was a month early. He thought he heard two heartbeats.

After hours of no-progress contractions, the fetal monitor showed the twins' distress, so they wheeled me from my labor room to the Obstetrical O.R., and lifted them out, about a minute apart.

My mother beamed. She said, *"God gave you two to make up for your trauma."*

I liked kids, but to me, they looked like him. They felt like his dirt, birthed from my wounds.

I tried to shake the feeling, and little by little, I warmed to their tiny, bird-like, open-mouthed rooting and their helpless dependence on me for their every moment's needs.

My mom' church did help, even with formula – though they were too cheap to spring for Pampers. I have to say, scrubbing newborn poop off of cloth diapers – times two – was really difficult on my still-touchy stomach.

They were not yet six months old when his lawyer's letter arrived.

The assailant, who had received only 8 years for the rapes, and non-fatal stabbings, of three strangers, was demanding a test to establish his paternity – and a judicial hearing to establish his custodial rights.

I was to bring the children to the designated location for medical examination.

They were, of course, *"his."*

Paternity established, from prison, a judge awarded him visitation. I was to update him by letter and send pictures of "his" children's progress over the next six months. And beginning with their first birthday, I was to bring them to the prison bi-weekly, for supervised visitation with their "father," until his release – either at the end of his sentence, or earlier, if he earned time off for good behavior.

If, after release, he, convinced the Court of his suitability, the Court would establish his paternal rights to joint legal and joint medical custody, and to unsupervised weekend visitations, holidays and vacation schedules – and to full residential custody, were I to predecease him during "his" children's minority.

By court order, the criminally-ill monster who had stolen my (and at least two other women's) sense of self and safety, and of cleanliness and ability to sleep through the night – or to simply walk to a car after dusk – had "the right" (and was to be trusted) to provide both my daughter – and my son – with their male parental role model (with no concern for *just what* he would model) – for life.

In the eyes of the court, they were equally "*his.*"

In the eyes of the court, this was in their "*best interest.*"

~ ~ ~

5. ABORTION IN RAPE

Parental "property" rights, and their impact on the failure of the courts to truly operate, with wisdom, in the best interests of child(ren), bring us back to the sole exception (sometimes) allowed by the Anti-Choice Movement – early-term **abortion on the grounds of rape or incest.**

Overwhelmingly, when a pregnancy is the result of rape[72] – **the rapist** is viewed by the family court system as *having rights*(!) to "*his* offspring" –

- *rights* to visitation – supervised, or **unsupervised** (!) – and/or

- *rights* to **joint custody** (joint legal, joint medical, and/or joint residential) – or

- even *rights* to **sole**[73] **custody** of the child(ren) **created by his**[74] **act(s) of sexual assault.**

And **his victim** – the child(ren)'s mother – **may be commanded** to transport her children (even to prison) to visit him (forcing her to see her assailant again, regularly) – or to turn her child(ren) over to her rapist for, and pick them up from him after, his custodial time.

---

[72] Defined as non-consensual penile-vaginal intercourse
[73] If the mother is ruled unfit, or predeceases her rapist, etc.
[74] While women* are able to commit sexual assault, people born with ova and uteri CANNOT impregnate another woman* (person born with ova and a uterus) by the act of rape – so the pronoun used here does, intentionally, designate people born with testes and penises (no matter their gender identity).

And this, even for **convicted rapists** – the overwhelming majority of whom are stranger rapists.

And this, even for **stranger** rapists convicted of the rape that caused the impregnation.

Most convicted rapists *are* stranger rapists (22% of rapists), as acquaintance rapists, overwhelmingly, do not go to prison.

Most acquaintance rapists (78% of rapists) do not even go to trial, as most acquaintance rape cases are difficult to prove in court – and are therefore declared "unfounded" (*which is not the legal equivalent of "untrue" – but rather indicates that the district attorney cannot predict with certainty that, under the rules of the current system, the case can be won, and therefore – opts out of prosecuting*).

In our system, sexual assault **victims do <u>not</u> *press charges*** against perpetrators.

It is the State – the police, and then, the district attorney – who make that judgment call, reducing the victim (when the D.A. does decide to prosecute) to a mere ***witness for* the State**.

And – rape is a crime of opportunity that, generally, happens without witnesses.

Which – from a legal perspective, means that *most* cases don't meet the threshold of evidence necessary for a D.A. (a lawyer who needs a record of career "wins") to decide to take them to court. Instead, assaults committed in the dark, and without witnesses, by persons the victim "knows," are dismissed as mere "he said/she said"[75] disputes about intent.

Overwhelmingly, the assailants the D.A. chooses to prosecute are the strangers who lay in wait in the bushes, wielding a weapon, leaving bruises, wounds, and scars.

Therefore, it is not surprising that, in the United States, an estimated 97% of rapes go unpunished in our legal system.[76]

So, if you are raped in the United States, understand – it is highly unlikely that your assailant will be prosecuted.

And understand that, even if your rapist is prosecuted, convicted, and sentenced – if you are impregnated by that rape – in our family court system – if your rapist pursues them – on DNA test, his "paternal" "**rights**" will be upheld and enforced.

Even when the physical violence against his victim is severe, it is highly unlikely the rapist's "paternal" "*rights*" will be severed.

So, if you are impregnated by rape and choose (or are forced) to carry to term, know and understand that your assailant (whether prosecuted or unprosecuted, and even if prosecuted and convicted) will be able, at any time, to demand his intact paternal parental "rights" – even from behind bars.

He will have the option – across your child(ren)'s minority – to establish and exercise his "father's" "*rights*" to "parental" visitation – and/or

---

[75] While not all rape is by men, and not all rape is of women, 78% - 80% of rape in the U.S. is by cisgender male acquaintances against cisgender females (dates/friends/relatives).
[76] 97% of rapists will never spend even a single day in jail," "98% of reported rapes are true, only 2% are false." TheOrderOfTheWhiteFeather. [accessed] 24 Aug 2016. *Rape Culture and Statistics*. https://wearawhitefeather.wordpress.com/survivors/rape-culture-statistics/

custody – and, as the "father," would be the first guardian of choice (despite whomever you may designate) in the event of your untimely death.

In all likelihood, you will not be able to prove him a rapist, and even if you can – *even if he were the violent stranger in the bushes with the knife who wounded you sufficiently for the D.A. to chose to prosecute*[77] – he will still be able – from prison – to petition the court to have you bring "his" child(ren) to him for visitation (thus exposing your young child(ren) to the prison environment and to the self-concept of being the child(ren) of a convicted rapist) – and upon his release – to seek unsupervised time with them alone – or joint or sole custody.[78]

You could be forced to see him, over and over, across your lifespan. And you can be forced to give him access to the child(ren) he "helped" create, via rape.

In that event, he:

1. will function both as your son(s) and/or daughter(s) role model of masculinity and fatherhood

and he, a rapist,

2. will have *sexual* access to them – according to his desires – across their entire *childhood(s) and adolescence* (across their minority)

---

[77] In our legal system, it is not the victim of rape, but the district attorney who decides whether or not to prosecute cases of sexual assault – and it is the police officers who first respond who have the discretion of whether or not to turn the case over to the district attorney's office. In the unlikely event a case goes to court, the rape victim, no matter their gender, is in the role of a witness for the state – not a plaintiff.

[78] Nolan, Caitlin. 9 Mar 2016. *Pregnant Through Rape, Women are Forced to Share Child Custody With Their Attackers.* InsideEdition.com. http://www.insideedition.com/headlines/15130-pregnant-through-rape-women-are-forced-to-share-child-custody-with-their-attackers; Hall, Katy & Chris Spurlock. 26 Jan 2013. *Worst States for Pregnant Rape Victims* (Infographic). HuffingtonPost.com. http://www.huffingtonpost.com/2013/01/26/pregnant-rape-abortion_n_2552183.html

The courts are unlikely to protect you – or them.

In regard to visitation and/or custody – as with demonstrated abusers[79]:

- there is **simply no discussion** in the public, or in the criminal justice sphere, **about the *ethics*** – or the kind of *gender role ideology* – that a man who impregnates a girl or woman by rape **will likely pass on:**

  - to either a daughter,

  - or a son.[80]

Or of whether or not someone who already impregnated a woman by rape,

- might be **more likely** than another parent **to rape the child** thus created.

Recently, some, but not all, states have passed *Rape Survivor Child Custody Acts*[81] that will allow women *in those states* – **who have the *financial***

---

[79] those who are physically and sexually abusive of their child(ren), or their child(ren)'s other parent

[80] As the man who raped his mother, how will he teach a son to view women? through what lens will he teach a daughter to see herself, and her own worth?

[81] "In May 2015, the Justice for Victims of Trafficking Act was enacted by Congress. Title IV of that act, the Rape Survivor Child Custody Act, increases the amount of STOP formula grant funding under the Violence Against Women Act (U.S.C. 3796gg *et seq.*) for those states that have a law **permitting mothers** of children conceived through rape **to seek termination of parental rights of their rapists**. [*NOTE: This termination is not automatic upon conviction. It requires the mothers to have the funds to go to court to "seek termination."] In addition, state legislatures have taken up the issue. Approximately 34 states and the District of Columbia have enacted legislation regarding the parental rights of perpetrators of sexual assault.

resources – **and for whom the state has been successful at proving their charge of rape in court** (a minute fraction of rape victims)[82] – to petition the court for the loss of the rapist's paternal rights – but only to the child created by the rape (not, in the case of an ex, to any other children he may have created with her). (*Given the level of proof necessary to secure conviction, and the reflection on character that committing rape is, I question why, upon conviction of rape, a rapist's paternal rights to the offspring of that rape, and to any other children he may have, are not automatically severed by the state without the necessity of petition from the victim. How the State can ever view a convicted rapist as a "fit" parent is incomprehensible.*)

Therefore, even this new measure is only of value in the protection of the very limited number of children, born of a stranger rape of which the perpetrator has actually been convicted – and in which the mother has the legal, financial, and emotional resources to take her assailant to court to block his custody.

Twenty-two states **allow for** termination of parental rights **if** the parent was convicted of sexual assault **which resulted in the birth of the child.** [So if your children's father were convicted of rape, in a rape that did not result in a pregnancy, his rights to your other children could not be terminated on the grounds of his being a convicted rapist. . . .] The other 12 states and the District of Columbia deny **or restrict** custody or visitation *if* the child was conceived as a result of a rape or sexual assault. Generally, **a conviction is required before parental rights are terminated.**" [So, this is of no value where the D.A. does not prosecute, and win. Remember, in rape trials, the victim is only a witness for the state, and is treated, by the rapist's defense lawyer, as if she is the one on trial – as the entire defense generally rests upon the "nuts or sluts" defense -- proving her "a liar" or a woman of "questionable character" who may have been "asking for it."] NCSL.org. 28 Jan 2016. *Parental Rights and Sexual Assault.* National Conference of State Legislators. http://www.ncsl.org/research/human-services/parental-rights-and-sexual-assault.aspx
[82] For whom the D.A. has chosen to, and successfully, prosecuted the assailant.

The overwhelming majority of children conceived by rape, and of women impregnated by rape, who choose to carry[83] to viability, will not be benefited by these acts.

Helping women who choose to carry to term, to protect their children from the influence, role modeling, and potential sexual predation of their rapist *children's progenitor* will require an entire paradigm shift in our criminal justice system – and in our cultural rape myths. Right now, societally, we **cannot even see** the **rights of women** to be protected from their assailant – or the rights of the child(ren) of rape to grow up without the unhealthy, potentially highly-destructive, influence of their rapist-progenitor.

Instead, the courts see women victims as **"exaggerants"** and fathers' as having **rights of access** to *their seed*.

Given the height of the bar for legal conviction, if anything should invalidate a man for fatherhood, it should be being convicted – of rape – or of being a sex offender against children – even their own.

---

[83] Often, despite the horror and violence done them, women will see the conception as innocent of that violence. There are any number of reasons a woman pregnant by rape may choose to carry, including being morally opposed to abortion, and/or unsure of being able to conceive again at a later date, and being **ignorant of the enforceable paternal rights of their assailant** to custody/visitation.

~~~

Clandestine Hole-in-the-Wall

A Narrative

They had a sort of sex ed in my high school. I had started in Catholic school, but by high school, I was in a relatively-elite Methodist school. My parents cared about education, and they cared about me. They wanted the best for me. We were solidly middle-class, but the tuition was always a small struggle. They told me, *"You are every bit as good as everyone there, but we won't be taking the kinds of vacations your classmates do."* In the 1980s, many of the more elite kids traveled, each summer, to Disney World, Orlando. To Brazilians, such a trip was quite expensive. We were fine, but we didn't have it like that.

Our sex ed class talked about the basics of reproduction. There were sketches of how the internal organs of each sex were shaped. But there was no contraceptive information. Condoms were available in drug stores, but it would have been humiliating for a girl to walk in, pick up a pack, and buy them. She would have been slut-shamed. Later on, and as a full adult aware of the need for safer sex, I would become the woman who had a condom in her purse, and who said, *"You're going to wear this,"* to a partner. But not at 17.

My mother though, had come to me, and said, *"Sex is good. But if you decide to begin having sex, I want you to come to me. I'll take you to the doctor and get you birth control. You just have to tell me."* But I hadn't. Somehow, I couldn't say that to mom.

Marcos was my first real boyfriend. He wasn't a one-night stand. He was a real, long-term boyfriend, the kind you think about having a life with. The kind you want to marry. I was a senior in high school, and he was three years older – an engineering student already working in an internship. But it was a time when no one had a consciousness of safe sex. Not in Brazil. In the early '80s, information had drifted in from the

States about GRID,[84] and then the terminology had changed to HIV[85] and AIDS,[86] but in my mind, and in the minds of all those I knew, that only affected gay people, and addicts who used needles, and hemophiliacs. . . . It didn't have anything to do with straight people, especially not with a young straight couple enthralled in their first real love affair.

And every other sexually transmissible disease of which I was aware was curable with a simple antibiotic. There was no talk of Herpes or HPV[87] either. So we had sex, unprotected.

As for pregnancy, somehow, I didn't really think it could happen to me. In the arrogance of my youthfulness, I didn't think I was fertile. Or I wondered about it. I just didn't feel like it could happen *to me*. I had plans!

Not going to college was not an option. I just knew I was going to college. Steady boyfriend, or no, I had career plans. Marrying Marcos was somewhere far down the timeline in those plans.

At first, I didn't realize I was pregnant. Not until I missed my period. Even then, it took me a few days to think anything of it. But I started to notice the very telling, small changes in my body. Almost immediately, my stomach had a small bump. And my breasts got tender in a way they hadn't been. And the shampoo I used every morning, the smell of it, started to make me nauseous.

When I started to worry, Marcos had an aunt who worked as a nurse, and she helped me find a doctor. This was before you could walk into a drug store and pick up a pregnancy test. You had to actually go to a gynecologist to be "diagnosed" as pregnant. The doctor ordered a blood test, and when I went back for the results, he told me I was "very" pregnant, about 4 weeks.

---

84 Gay-Related Immune Deficiency
85 Human Immunodeficiency Virus
86 Acquired Immune Deficiency Syndrome
87 Human Papillomavirus

He offered me no options. Knowing I was 17, he didn't ask if I needed help telling my parents. He didn't discuss adoption. He simply told me, matter-of-factly, and let me walk out of there, completely unprepared for what I was facing.

Marcos and I began to talk about what we could do. His sister, about two years older than him, began to tell us to just get married. But I wanted to finish high school. And I had to go to college.

I was suffused in a whirlwind of conflicting feelings. I had always been pro-choice, but somewhere in the midst of all my emotions, I let myself wonder *if it would be a girl or a boy*. Then I would stop myself and think, *"But I am just a kid myself."*

I've always been a very rational person. Even then, at 17, I was quite rational. I asked myself, *"How could I have a kid, and raise a kid, before I was prepared to care for a kid?"*

Marcos was wonderfully supportive. He was a really good boyfriend. I don't know how I would have made it through that time without his emotional, and at times, physical (as in physically holding me up) support. He kept saying, *"Whatever you decide, I'll help you through this."* And he did.

There seemed so little we could do. Abortion was illegal – nationwide. It was a Catholic country. It was a misogynistic country. It was a machismo country. Getting pregnant was considered to be the woman's fault. If unmarried, she was shamed, and she was supposed to pay the social price. A woman caught and convicted of an illegal abortion faced jail time. As a nation, we were just out from under a military dictatorship. We actually, finally, had a civilian in the position of oversight. Not an elected civilian, but a civilian nonetheless.[88] In that time and place, women had few rights.

---

[88] Today, in Brazil, "access to safe, legal abortions is severely restricted." "Well before the rise of Zika, there were as many as 900,000 illegal abortions in Brazil each year." (McDonald, Brent. 18 May 2016. *Brazil's Abortion Restrictions Compound Challenge of Zika Virus.* New York Times. https://www.nytimes.com/2016/05/19/world/americas/zika-virus-abortion-brazil.html

I decided not to carry, but we had to be very careful. I told no one. Marcos told his aunt, and an older man at work, who knew a place. . . . It was super clandestine, a real hole-in-the-wall.

But we didn't have the money. For us, the price was huge. And we didn't have much time either. I was already 4 to 5 weeks pregnant. We scrambled for that money. We really, really, got creative, raising the funds for my down-low abortion.

My dad had a retail store. My parents knew and liked Marcos. I told my dad we wanted to go to the beach and needed to make money for the trip. He offered me branded t-shirts and sweatshirts, and I sold some at school. While going through his stock for things to sell, we found new, blank VHS cassettes he had picked up in the States, and he let us have those. People were all about them. They wanted them to tape their TV shows.

Marcos sold some at work, and he told two of his cousins about our problem, and they pitched in, and helped us sell. As a male, he didn't feel the shame I felt – the shame of being 17, unmarried, and pregnant. The shame of being female and in the eyes of critics (if they found out) no longer "chaste." To this day, thirty-years later, I have never told my parents. I never wanted to soooo disappoint them like that.

The only person I ever told, other than Marcos' aunt, was my own aunt, my mother's sister, about one month after my procedure. She looked at me funny and, in private, asked, *"Are you pregnant?"* So I told her, *"No, I had an abortion,"* even as I begged, *"Please don't tell my mom."* I don't think she ever did, but if she did, my mom's an even better secret keeper than me, because she's never said a word to me. Also, I sometimes think about how, when I left home to go to college, I left my room set up, and in that room was my diary where I had chronicled the whole experience. I sometimes wonder if my mom ever went through my things, ever found or read that journal. But again, I won't ask, and if she did, she didn't tell.

Whatever happened to us – unplanned pregnancy, sexual assault, domestic violence – it was always, and only, a woman's fault. We shouldn't have opened our legs. . . We shouldn't have dressed that way. . . We shouldn't have pissed him off. . . .

It took about two weeks, but with my dad's merchandise and Marco's cousins' help, we raised the money that a 17-year-old high school kid and a 20-year-old intern just didn't have on their own.

Marco's went with me, on the bus. I remember, he couldn't come back with me into the treatment room.

I remember not liking the feel of the place. I remember there was a female nurse or assistant of some kind, but she wasn't in the room for my exam, and I don't know if she was there for the procedure, once I was under.

I remember the examination table, and the stirrups, and the man between my legs with a bright lamp. I remember glancing around the room, seeing the vacuum aspirator, wondering if he were about to use that on me. I remember the doctor saying he would put me under general anesthesia. I remember my driving need for this to hurry up and be over – both the pregnancy – and the procedure.

The next thing I remember, I was still half asleep, and I was being led out the door. I can't remember the clinic having any concern for me after it was done. *Was it even a clinic?*

There was no recovery room. I was simply put out on the street. Marcos steadied me, and we rode the bus back to his place, me propped up against him, mostly asleep. I would not have been able to get home – alone.

We had told my parents that we went to the beach. In actuality, we spent the weekend at his parents' house, as they were away for the weekend.

About two days later, I began to have the most horrible cramps. I literally thought they would kill me. It felt like someone was twisting my ovaries and uterus in a giant hand. The pain got so bad, Marcos had to take me back to the clinic, where I explained how I was feeling, and the doctor told me I *had a blood clot in there*, and would *have to be put under again to have the clot removed*.

Again, I let him put me under general anesthesia. I look back and shudder, realizing I had no idea of the sanitation of the place, the antiseptic status of the equipment, or the ethics of the doctor. As far as I know, no one was with me, no other medical staff, to keep him from abusing me. I don't have any indication that he did, but there also weren't any of the standard measures in place to assure that he didn't.

And was it a blood clot? Or had he failed to remove all of the embryonic and placental tissue the first time around?

And I had no options. There weren't any other "clinics" to choose from. Maybe women with more money might have had higher class options, but we had one solitary tip, from the older man at Marcos' internship, pointing out where to go for an illegal, necessarily clandestine, procedure that could have put either me, the patient, or the doctor, in legal jeopardy of prison.

And there was no Internet. There was no way to do research. You hinted at people, and if they hinted back, you followed the clues to fill in the puzzle, and hoped you succeeded at ending your unwanted pregnancy, surviving whatever was done to you, and not getting caught.

Marcos and I broke up some time later, not because of the pregnancy or the abortion, but because our lives moved on. I went on to college as he left college and moved forward in his career. There are times a three-year age gap is small, and times it looms large. For us, it did us in.

But we kept in touch, and one day, not so long ago, he sent me the news that the doctor who had done my procedure had been arrested for having killed two women in their abortions. He's currently serving 10 to 15 years.

After my abortion, I went on the pill and took it steadfastly for 20 years. Marcos married and had one child. I completed college, began my career, married, went to graduate school; then, super-late in my 30s, started to try to have a family. By then, it was hard for me to get pregnant. My fertility specialist said I have a *"tight cervix." Is my botched first, or my second follow-up, procedure to blame for that?*

My husband and I did five rounds of In Vitro Fertilization. All five failed. In Vitro is a whole other kind of suffering for a woman – the harvesting of the eggs, and the implantation, made especially painful by a "tight cervix". . . .

But I thank God because, actually, my husband was an asshole, and I'm grateful, now, not to be bound to him by children. If I had had children with him, I might not even be able to be in this country. In our divorce, he could have controlled my living arrangements and career, in order to have access to "his" children.

In my mind, the entire history of my reproductive health has to do with the fact that the abortion I accessed at 17-years-old was neither safe nor legal. It has taken me these 30 years to come to terms with the repercussions of having to seek out a hole-in-the-wall, back alley, abortionist who likely failed to fully evacuate my uterus the first time around – a man who went on to be convicted of killing two patients. It was a journey to Hell, for sure.

On the other hand, I have, and have always had, a clear stance on a woman's right to choose.

No man has a right to have a say. Men don't have to carry. Men don't have to labor. And if they want, men can simply walk away.

It is the woman whose body is used, and it is her life trajectory that is inalterably changed.

If we had not done the abortion, Marcos might have married me. And that would have impacted his career as well.

But if I had not had the abortion, I could not have walked away. I would not have given my child up for adoption, and it would have been ten or more years before I could ever have gone to college. I would have been a despised teenage mom, probably single, struggling to feed a child I couldn't afford.

If I had kept the baby, would I have resented it?

If Marco had married me, would he have resented me? Resented the baby?

Would I have come to resent him?

In retrospect, I am still terrified at what my life would have been, if I, married or unmarried, had had a kid at 17-years-old, because I couldn't have accessed an abortion at all.

And I am terrified at the kind of abortion I was forced to access – illegal, unsafe, potentially unsanitary, potentially-deadly.

I have never felt any Catholic guilt about having "killed" my child. I know it was an early embryo, and I could not have, then, given it the life it deserved. I am terrified at how close I came to bringing into the world one more unwanted, under-attended child, who could have grown up – messed up – with that pain.

I believe in the necessity of choice. I believe only the woman can make that choice. I have never regretted my choice, only my lack of safe options, free from shame. And I find it terrifying that here, in the United States, the Religious Right is not only chiseling away at women's abortion rights, but at women's access to contraception itself – while in my native, Catholic, Brazil, abortion remains unsafe and illegal, but the birth control pill is available, at the drug story, over-the-counter.

And I am thankful that I did not die on that back alley abortionist's table, either time I had to lie there for the same abortion.

~ ~ ~

6. FEMALE-CONTROL OF CONTRACEPTION

& EARLY-TERM ABORTION

Counseling mothers and children through these machinations, I have begun to understand the enormity of women* not being able to control their own reproduction – the effects it has on their (and their children's) lives – to be pregnant when they do not want to be – and/or

- at the wrong time – and/or

- by the wrong man.*

As a woman, as a family member, as an ordained minister, as a spiritual counselor – I have become witness to the crying need for:

- easily accessible and affordable *female-controlled* [89] contraception

    o and for males to *make use of* their own *male-controlled* contraception/STI protection

---

[89] Males should also make sure that they are not making children they don't want, with women with whom they don't want to be partnered long-term. Males already have *some* male-controlled contraception – condoms (and vasectomy). Perhaps, in the future, they will discover a hormonal contraception for men. But even if they do, because it is bodies with ovaries and wombs that host and carry fetuses, people with those bodies will still have a special need to have contraception they can faithfully use, in the interest of their own autonomous choices about reproduction.

And when contraception fails, for:

- reliable access to emergency contraception (the morning-after pill, which is not an abortifacient), and when that fails, for

- autonomous access to

    o safe, legal, early-term medical abortion[90]

    o safe, legal, first-trimester surgical abortion [91]

And when there are fetal anomalies, for:

- later-term (generally second-trimester) abortion

Or when, before fetal viability, the mother is at medical risk of imminent death:

- later-term (also, generally still second-trimester)[92] abortion

---

[90] Works 94 to 98% of the time in the first 8 weeks, 94 to 96% of the time in weeks 8 through 9, 91 to 93% of the time in weeks 9 through 10, 87% of the time in weeks 10 through 11. https://www.plannedparenthood.org/learn/abortion/considering-abortion/what-facts-about-abortion-do-i-need-know

[91] 1 in 3 to 1 in 4 women will have an abortion by age 45. "Abortion is safe. Unless there's a rare and serious complication that's not treated, there's no risk to your ability to have children in the future or to your overall health. Having an abortion doesn't increase your risk for breast cancer, and it doesn't cause depression or mental health issues. Abortions don't cause infertility either. In fact, it's possible to get pregnant quickly after you have an abortion. So it's a good idea to talk to your nurse or doctor about a birth control plan for after your abortion." https://www.plannedparenthood.org/learn/abortion/considering-abortion/what-facts-about-abortion-do-i-need-know

[92] Third trimester abortions are very infrequent. Legally, they are used onlly in cases of severe fetal anomaly, that will inhibit the length and quality of life of the fetus. There are almost no providers, and they are extremely expensive. They are not legal "on demand." That is intentional misinformation.

*Note – When, to save the life and health of the mother, immediate delivery is necessary (as in preeclampsia/eclampsia), fetuses that have reached potential viability (24 to 28 weeks[93]) **are given the best chance at life. They are NOT aborted. They are delivered** (generally by Caesarian Section) **to NICU [Intensive Care].**[94] **[Full term is 39 to 40 weeks.]**

As for the effect it has on children's lives, bringing a child into the world is an enormous responsibility, and to do so in less than ideal circumstances – to bring a child into the world that you cannot care for physically/ emotionally/ intellectually – is a wrong the Anti-Choice Movement does not want to grapple with intellectually.

Contraception is not as simple as a woman, "keeping her legs shut."

For one, keeping "her legs shut" is not always up to her.

When she is raped, yes, but also – beyond the realm of what most of us would class as rape – a woman in an abusive relationship is often :

- deprived, by her abusive partner, of the right to time their intercourse (to say yes or no according to her inclination, health, or fertility cycle), and/or

- denied, by her controlling partner, access to hormonal birth control, and may also

---

[93] Fetal viability WITH intensive care: is 24 weeks/6 months) to 28 weeks /7 months – or **the third trimester.**
[94] The Neonatal Intensive Care Unit

- be deprived, at his will, of his condom use.[95]

Knowledge about, and untroubled access to, a female-controlled[96] form of contraception is often the only way for a woman to be sure she does not end up with the choice of whether to bring a child (another child) into a fraught situation, or to prevent (through the morning-after pill), or to terminate as quickly as possible (through medication, while it is still a blastocyst or a pre-fetal embryo, or surgically).

There are a myriad of situations in which a woman can find herself, when luck does not go her way, from:

- being pregnant when she does not want to be

- to having difficulty conceiving

- to having offspring that face a range of challenges

As a rational human being, I have come to know that the life (and the quality of life) of the mother (and the *quality* of the life of the viable[97] fetus) matter as much, or more, than the zygote, blastocyst, or embryo. I know that an embryo is not yet a developed, or an independent, life, and that the cost to the potential mother (no matter how wanted or unwanted a child would be) may be simply staggering (and if carried to viability, the life of an unwanted, or seriously ill, child may be hellish and debilitating).

---

[95] Lori L. Heise. 1997. *Violence, Sexuality, and Women's Lives.* In Roger N. Lancaster & Micaela di Leonardo. The Gender Sexuality Reader: Culture, History, Political Economy. New York: Routledge. (pp.411-433).
[96] Women in abusive relationships often find the way to fund and take hormonal contraceptives on the downlow from their partners. Also, for those who can access contraception in ways that won't show on a husband's medical insurance bills, methods like the IUD may be relatively undetectable.
[97] 24 week or older fetus

~ ~ ~

The Right to the Right

A Narrative

When I woke up that morning, my breasts sort of ached. The feeling was vague, but as the week progressed, it came to remind me of the way my breasts felt when they first developed – achy – and painfully sensitive to the touch. As a preteen, I had roller-skated into the shoulder of an empty wire coat hanger. We had a tile-covered playroom, empty of real furniture, and it was raining outside; so I keyed on my skates and sailed across the open floor space, only to run – front-first – into a standing clothes rack at the far end of the rectangular room – and the pain of the tip of that one empty wire hanger, mid-nipple, had made me double-over.

Suddenly, they felt like that again – like even air was bothersome and a poke would bring me to my knees.

And my belly. My waistband bothered me – the pressure was unpleasant, the denim of my well-worn jeans, confining.

I hadn't noticed that my period hadn't come. It was erratic anyway, and we didn't have apps back then. Just a hanging wall calendar in the kitchen, and it always felt too public to chart my cycle there – for everyone else to see.

It was only when the tenderness in my breasts made me start to wonder if something were medically wrong, that I made an appointment with a gynecologist.

Pregnant. By his best calculation, 6 weeks along.

The weight of it sank like a stone into my chest. I wasn't in love with JerMaine. We had known each other forever, since middle school actually. And we had been boyfriend and girlfriend through high school. But those were pre-sexual years, and we hadn't actually lost our virginity with each other. Instead, we kissed, and held hands, and cuddled, and sometimes "petted," but each of our pants always stayed on; and then, college had split us up. He went his way, and I went mine. He headed South, to a historic Black university, and I headed to a New England school that had been admitting African American students for more than a century. And we grew apart.

It was the '70s, and the Free Love movement was on, and by then, neither of us were virgins any longer – so sometimes, on winter and summer breaks, we got together.

But I wasn't in love with him. And I couldn't see him being a good father. I had just graduated, and he was finishing up, but he liked his recreational drug use too much – his weed, his Quaaludes, his cocaine. . . .

And he had a temper. . . . And an edge of control, whenever he thought my guard was down (which wasn't very often)!

And none of this was in my plans!

I was working two jobs: in my field, teaching art to grade school children, and waitressing; and on break, as a waitress and a lifeguard down the shore. I was looking forward to another summer on the beach – young – and carefree.

And with graduation pending, my applications were already out for grad school the following fall.

A baby just wasn't in my plans.

JerMaine was always good at withdrawal. I didn't think he had failed to pull out in time. But the doctor said live sperm can leak in pre-ejaculate, and I should have been on the pill.

I spent the next two weeks agonizing.

I'm a very logical person. Very analytical. And it wasn't like me to be indecisive, but I have to admit to 12 to 14 days of cognitive shock. I was having trouble thinking it through.

But I knew who to call. My sister was like me. She had a good head on her shoulders, and I could trust her to steer me in the right direction – or at least, to break me out of my stall.

I have the best family. Really supportive. All anyone could ask for. Brenda reached right through the phone and let me know I had it within me to make the right decision. She said, "Get some paper. Make a list – pros and cons. You'll know what to do."

There was only a single entry on the pro side – a potential baby.

I actually dreamt of motherhood. I looked forward to being a mother – someday – after I was established. . . . After my master's. After my career was moving forward – so I could care for, and support, a child. . . .

The con list was long.

The timing was wrong. Even at 22, part of me knew that I was still too young. I wanted to experience each stage of life. I didn't want to be robbed of my youth on my way to responsibility.

The father was wrong. I didn't trust the person I was with – not to parent. I didn't trust him to get himself together *for this potential life*. Despite our long friendship, there were some things in his childhood he just hadn't worked through. His immaturity – the likelihood he would never grow up, or would live his adulthood hooked – made me not want him as an influence on any child I might have. I could see addiction settling into its long-term hold.

And I knew he wouldn't pull it together for *me*. . . .

So, I made my decision. It was simply logical. This was not the time. I would take care of this and be more careful going forward.

I told my mom, and she let me know she had my back. She let me share my reasons, then let me know, "*Whatever I decided, I would always be **her** baby.*"

I didn't tell my father, but we talked about it later, matter-of-factly, in front of him. Despite their devout Christianity, it was just never an issue with my family.

The morning of my procedure, I was calm. I quietly drove myself to the clinic. It was clean, professional – and legal. The staff was kind and efficient, and my doctor was Black , too.

As I waited, the teenage girl on the gurney next to me began to sob. I got off my cart and went to comfort her. I listened, then assured her that her mother was right. She was much too young to become a mother herself. She could do this again, later. Before she had a baby, she should finish her education, and make sure she was independent and could take care of a child. Waiting now would be a gift to the children she had.

The nurse chased me back to my gurney, but as we waited, we lay there looking at each other, and it felt like Divine Providence that I was there for her, like she took comfort from my strength.

In surgery, they anesthetized my cervix. All I felt was a sensation of tugging. And, quickly, it was over.

When they released me from Recovery, I drove home in my aging green Toyota Celica, stepping on the clutch and shifting gears the whole way. I crawled into my mother's bed, and she held me as I fell asleep. I stayed two days, then got back to my life.

I never rethought my decision. I didn't ponder it again, and I've never regretted it; maybe because I had so much family support, or maybe because I have an analytical nature. The pro and con list had helped me determine the right decision – for me.

That fall, I entered graduate school. I completed my master's, then moved up in the school system, building a career I loved – teaching children, and finally, becoming an administrator. Over the years, I've helped many, many children find their way in life.

And a few years later, I determined that it was the right time for me to have that baby, and got pregnant by choice. My son is the pride and joy of my life. His only competition for my heart is the grandbaby he and his partner have given me.

But even pregnant with him, I determined that the right choice for me was to not get married – so I raised him on my own – and my economic independence was critical to the quality of life I was able to give to him.

Today, he stands, a proud father, with his own undergrad and graduate degrees from HBCU's, that I was able to help fund, under his belt.

When JerMaine found out I'd had the abortion, with that edge of control I'd intuited, he told me I should have asked him first.

I told him that it wasn't his body – that he didn't have to carry for nine months, or give birth, or go through postpartum recovery – or even be a solid parent for two decades – that as a male, he could even have left me to do it all, or worse, stayed – and messed up our child with his addictions.

I find it hard to believe that, in today's political climate, we are back in this fight – back in the time even before I had my abortion – back In my mother's day – back in an era in which a woman's right to choose a safe abortion – or even to try to prevent pregnancy – is again under assault.

And through the years I've often wondered how the girl I met that day, on the other gurney, turned out. *What life did she live? Did God bring me there, that day, as much for her as for me?*

~ ~ ~

7. THE TRIMESTER APPROACH TO
THE (Female*)[98] CITIZEN'S RIGHT TO PRIVACY

The Supreme Court ruled in Roe v. Wade, that while paternal rights do belong to fathers **after birth**, early pregnancy is not the place for father's rights. Because the physical rigors of pregnancy are **borne on one side of the sexed divide, only** – and no matter how involved or sympathetic – not on the other – in the first few weeks or months, the decision to carry, or to terminate, a new pregnancy must be in the hands of the individual woman or girl (person-with-a-uterus), as it is she alone (if a human newborn is to result) that must play host throughout the developmental process – and go through the processes of labor and delivery. It is also she who will, most likely, be saddled with the lion's share of the childcare – across the ensuing two decades.

On those grounds, the Supreme Court ruled that the person with the gestational organs has the **right to privacy** in regard to the decisions she makes over her own body – about gestation.

To be blunt, in the (non-medical) creation of a child, the *person with the*

---

[98] For purposes of this discussion, sex assigned on the basis of the internal reprouctive organs that can be impregnated – the uterus and the egg-bearing ova, with or against the female* will

sperm has an orgasm[99] (and may, if he deigns, contribute financially and/or emotionally).

In the creation of a child, the *reproductive partner with the uterus* – with or without having achieved orgasm – begins to go through changes to her own body that include some combination of:

- morning sickness

- swollen breasts

- sore breasts

- extremes of tiredness and sleepiness in the middle of the workday

- very frequent urination
    - that repetitively interrupts work
    - that repetitively interrupts each night's sleep

- swelling of the feet and ankles

- weight gain

- increasing indigestion

- gastric reflux

- loss of calcium to the teeth and bones

- nutritional-depletion

- eventually-continuous back pain

- potential swelling of the hands and face

- inability to reach one's feet to tie one's own shoes

- late-term difficulty walking (hormones soften ligaments, so the pelvis can expand to pass the neonate vaginally)

- and, more seriously, if things are not going so well:

---

[99] Or at least, leaks live sperm inside or near the vaginal opening

- o   gestational diabetes, hypertension and/or preeclampsia
- and finally, labor (lasting anywhere from 2 to 72+[in the third world] hours)
  - o   and/or Cesarean section (planned or emergency) with its post-operative recovery
- and permanent stretch marks. . . .

I know, experientially, that – at some level – each time a woman carries and delivers, she takes some risk to her own life.

In the realm of civil rights, of citizen's rights in a secular democracy, forced maternity is not something that we can, rightly, demand of any woman.

~ ~ ~

We Gave Birth to Joy

A Narrative

I didn't want to have a baby alone. My biological clock was ticking, but I couldn't do it alone. I had a good job. Had enough to cover daycare. Had enough to purchase some sperm. But I didn't want to do it alone. I had no family in the country. No mother or aunts or sisters or close cousins who could step in and help me shoulder the burdens of early childcare.

On the other hand, I couldn't imagine a childless old age. And while I had gotten to 38 without a child, I wanted a baby. I, even, longed for a baby. I ached to hold one in my arms – craved the smell of baby shampoo on a newly-washed infant scalp.

All along, I dated. The further I got into my 30s, the more serious my dating became to me. I was past the age where I could easily meet men. High school and college were past. I had no "matchmaker" friends, and while many couples meet at work, I didn't have that kind of job. In the corporation – if you steer clear of your boss or supervisee – and the hierarchical threat of sexual harassment – sheer proximity can make romance bloom.

But not in my workplace. It was almost all female, and I'm not lesbian – not that there's anything wrong with that – but being attracted to men, it left me few opportunities.

Even more than I wanted a baby, I wanted a boyfriend, a lover, a man in whose arms I could fall asleep each night. And I wanted my child to arise from lovemaking – not from an injection of sperm in a doctor's office – not that there's anything wrong with that.

I wanted a man, who was man enough, to get out of bed at the 2 a.m. feeding and bring me our baby, so I could nurse without really having to wake up – a man in the delivery room (just like a movie husband) telling me to breathe, as our child crested its way into the world.

So I went online. It was the only place I had to meet a man. And it was a numbers game.

I slept with almost none of them. I was fishing for a big fish, and I didn't want to end up stuck with the first, or the second, small fish I found. So I dated, without bedding, unless a significant relationship developed. There were two of those along the way, but before we moved to marriage or childbearing, those relationships ended, and I searched on.

I set up a Google Voice number from an unconnected email (so the creeps couldn't stalk me) and pressed forward – reaching out, going on dates, tossing back the small fish, tending my hook.

The stories I could tell you of the men I tossed back. . . .

Really, Guys, *"What am I wearing?"* and *"Do I do anal?"* are not initial come-on lines! *They're about as repulsive as the Breather on the anonymous phone call . . . .*

I found a sea of creeps online, and a few real human beings – an occasional good guy.

There was the guy who had spent 6 years working for an NGO in Asia. He had such wonderful stories to tell, and there was so much in him to admire!

And there was the guy who worked for his father's construction company and had 60 immediate family members, each one warmer and kinder than the last.

But, at 45, the NGO guy, still working on his second master's, had nothing to show for his years of dedication but a load of student debt. And the son of the construction entrepreneur was incapable of making even a small decision, without the consensus of his enormous tribe.

Samuel was different.

No only did I find him attractive, which still really mattered, but he had a solid income and a house. We shared a financial philosophy about saving, and both of us cared intensely what our retirement would look like someday.

Like me, he was independent and adventurous, with his family at some distance, and we had fun on our dates. We liked to rock climb and hike. We went to book readings and plays. We had avid, sometimes heated, discussions about politics. And we fell in love.

It was time. The closer I got to 40, the freakier my gynecologist got about my plans. After a year of dating, it was time to try – even before the wedding, which we threw together quietly, once the test kit said, *Pregnant.*

Given my age, at 15 weeks, we had an ultrasound, and the genetic quad screen, checking for AFP, hCG, Estriol, and Inhibin-A.

Then came the first look at our baby! I forwarded her picture to everyone on our contact lists. The image on the ultrasound was a little otherworldly, but it was almost like you could tell what she looked like – or would look like.

Then, the quad screening came back abnormal.

Through my tears, my doctor assured me that *"everything might still be alright."* We *"wouldn't know for a few more weeks, but it could prove to be a "false positive." It's too early to tell,"* she reassured me. I *"just needed to breath deeply and hold on."* We *"would do further testing in a few weeks. In the meantime, my husband and I could think about what we would choose, if the second test confirmed the anomaly."*

They scheduled my amniocentesis.

At 20 weeks, and three days, we went in for the procedure. I was nervous. When I'd checked the mirror that morning, before the drive to the facility, my face had a little of that "deer in the headlights" look. I got through that day by simply following instructions. All those years, of obeying the nuns in grade school, kicked in. I just did as I was told. I took off this, and I put on that. I climbed up on the table. I reclined, but without relaxing.

My husband was determined to be there for me. They brought him a chair and made a space in the midst of all their equipment. He held my hand.

They squirted my belly with the conductive gel. As the images came up on the monitor, I thought about turning my face away, but I was riveted to the screen.

The ultrasound technician kept up a steady chatter. My husband chatted back, a little. She wanted to know, if we wanted to know, the sex. He nodded yes to her pointed inquiry, and as if underwater in a pool, I heard her say, *"It's a girl."* Then she found the pocket of fluid for the needle aspiration.

My doctor stepped up to the table, and with curt clinical conversation between them, they seemed to dance around my abdomen. There was the sanitizing swabbing of my skin and my doctor's warnings about the sensations I might experience. The piercing by the needle did sting, but it barely registered on my awareness. I tried not to flinch as the needle penetrated the uterine wall, but the cramped response was undeniable. I kept watching the screen, worried the baby would move and get pricked by the needle – willing the baby to be well.

An hour later, released, Samuel tried to turn into our favorite diner, but I – curled against the passenger doorframe – found myself unable to exit the car and sit among people.

Even though he hated them, he drove through the next fast-food place on our route home, and let me crawl, unimpeded, into our bed, and rock myself into a fitful sleep.

Sunday we went to church. The altar server rotation had shifted. That Sunday, there was an altar girl – with Down's Syndrome.

At each step, the priest, or the second altar girl, would take a moment and redirect her. That week, there was a parish meeting after 12 o'clock mass, and I watched her with her mother. She seemed high functioning, but I noticed that, despite the fact her body looked about 12, her comprehension seemed much, much younger; and her mom didn't get a moment's peace. She got her daughter a plate, but not one for herself. She took a bite of her daughter's food, then began feeding her. She followed her around, redirecting her interactions with others, steering her nearly-teen body to the restroom.

Pregnant, I had to use it about the same time. The mom never got to use the toilet. Even hand washing only proceeded under her steady reminders. *"Now, pull up your pants. Come over here. Turn the water on. Use the soap. No, don't coat the handles with the soap. Now rinse off the suds. Dry your hands. Use a paper towel on the door handle. Would you like more to eat before we go home?"*

It was clear. Her mom was never, would never, be off duty. She would never be off duty as long as she lived. Their family unit was never off duty. Even her younger brother was pressed into leading her around. She required constant attention, and she always would. She would age, but not mature. *What did she feel? What did she understand?*

As the church meeting ended, and the parishioners filed out to their cars, two waiting neighbor boys popped out of a row of evergreens that lined the church lot, to yell, *"Retard!"* at her and pelt her with pebbles.

For all of her mother's, and her family's, love and care, she wasn't safe in the world.

I thought how tired her mother looked.

I wondered, *What would happen to her when her mother aged and died?*

Did her mother know before giving birth? Had she done genetic testing? If knowing, she had chosen to bring her daughter into the world, was it the right choice? Was it fair to the child?

As her mother aged, would her younger brother grow into the burden of caregiving throughout her adulthood? Would it complicate his ability to go off to school, to work, to have a family of his own in ten or fifteen years?

When her parents predeceased her, would the daughter end her years in a group home? Would she be safe there, once her family could no longer monitor her every need?

The sinking feeling of dread about my own amnio grew.

I remembered the Down's Syndrome man I knew who'd been raped for years in a group home. Mentally-incapacitated, he hadn't been able to speak up for himself. The abuse only stopped when another staff member caught the perpetrator – another "caregiver" – in the act.

Could I endure never having my own life again?

I wanted a child. But I wanted a child who would mature and, perhaps, someday, be there for me.

Could I bring Grace (for after the ultrasound, we had named her) *into the world, to never know the joy of independence? To be led and guided, but never able to keep herself safe?*

And Samuel, *What was he thinking?*, for he had a part in this too. *What would we do if they confirmed the Down's?*

The doctor's call ended all doubt. She confirmed our worst fears. The fetus did have Down's.

We talked. We wept. We held each other. We knew.

We simply couldn't.

We considered the advancement of medical technology, to the stage where they could inform us of life-restricting abnormalities before birth, to be an act of God as well; and we accepted the grace of living in a time and place where there was a choice. And we chose to send her back into His care, instead of bringing her into a world where she would never thrive and would face an ongoing and overwhelming threat of mistreatment – a world in which we, as parents, could not give her a fair shot at keeping safe.

At week 23, still shy of fetal viability, we went in for our procedure. As per our doctor's instructions, we waited 12 weeks before again having unprotected sex. We conceived again, and this time, the amniocentesis came back perfect, and eighteen months after we conceived Grace, we gave birth to *Joy.*

~~~

8. RISKS OF PREGNANCY VS.

RISKS OF LEGAL & ILLEGAL ABORTION

In the case of an unwanted pregnancy, no one outside of that woman can demand that – because she had sex (voluntary or involuntary), and there was a failure of contraception (attempted or not attempted) – she *must* try to carry to term. The ways in which pregnancy takes over the host's body, and the real risks of medical complications it carries, do mandate the woman's right to privacy in this decision.

Even in the U.S., the maternal death rate is 18.5 deaths per 100,000 live births (2013),[100] with an ongoing racial disparity, unchanged across the last half-century, of African American to White women = 3.4 - 4.0:1.[101]

And globally:

> 800 women die every day from pregnancy or childbirth
> related causes." According to the United Nations
> Population Fund (UNFPA) this is equivalent to "about
> one woman every two minutes and for every woman who

---

[100] "Double the rate it was in 1979-1986 (of 9.1 per 100,000)" Wikipedia. *Maternal Death.* [last modified] 11 August 2016. https://en.wikipedia.org/wiki/Maternal_death
[101] King, M.D., Jeffrey C. *Maternal Mortality in the United States: Current Status* (PowerPoint). ACOG.org. https://www.acog.org/-/media/Departments/Public-Health-and-Social-Issues/Maternal-Mortality-In-The-US.pdf?la=en

dies, 20 or 30 encounter complications with serious or long-lasting consequences. . . . UNFPA estimated that 289,000 women died of pregnancy or childbirth related causes in 2013.[102]

Abortion also has risks, but "legal[103] abortion is actually far safer than childbirth and delivery" (and spares the *unwilling* host months and months of the gestational process, and an unwanted child to give care to for the whole of a childhood – or to give away and wonder about. . . .

Statistically, legal induced abortion is markedly safer than childbirth. In the U.S., "the mortality rate related to induced abortion was 0.6 deaths per 100,000 abortions."[104] The risk of death associated with childbirth is approximately 14 times higher than that with [legal] abortion."[105]

On the other hand, when we make abortion illegal, we make it unsafe:

According to the World Health Organization (WHO), every 8 minutes[106] a woman in a developing nation will die of complications arising from an unsafe abortion."("An *unsafe abortion* is defined as "a procedure for terminating an unintended pregnancy carried out either by persons lacking

---

[102] United Nations Population Fund. *Maternal Health.* [accessed] 20Aug 2016. http://www.unfpa.org/maternal-health

[103] *Unsafe* [illegal] abortion is another major cause of maternal death. According to the World Health Organization, every eight minutes a woman dies from complications arising from unsafe abortions. Complications include cervical tearing, perforated uterus/bowel/bladder, hemorrhage, infection, sepsis and genital trauma [11] Globally, preventable deaths from improperly performed procedures constitute 13% of maternal mortality, and 25% or more in some countries where maternal mortality from other causes is relatively low, making unsafe abortion the leading single cause of maternal mortality worldwide. https://en.wikipedia.org/wiki/Maternal_death

[104] Raymond EG, Grimes DA. 2012 Feb119 (2 Pt 1): 215-9. *The Comparative Safety of Legal Induced Abortion and Childbirth in the United States.* Obstetrics & Gynecology. PubMed.gov. http://www.ncbi.nlm.nih.gov/pubmed/22270271

[105] ibid

[106] "Every day, **approximately 830** women die from preventable causes related to pregnancy and childbirth." WHO.Int. Nov 2015. Maternal Mortality: Fact Sheet #348. Media Centre. World Health Organization. http://www.who.int/mediacentre/factsheets/fs348/en/

the necessary skills or in an environment that does not conform to minimal medical standards, or both.")[107]

And:

Every year, worldwide, about 42 million women with unintended pregnancies choose abortion, and *nearly half of these procedures*, 20 million, *are unsafe*. Some 68,000 women die of unsafe abortion annually, making it one of the leading causes of maternal mortality (13%). Of the women who survive unsafe abortion, 5 million will suffer long-term health complications. Unsafe abortion is thus a pressing issue. Both of **the primary methods for preventing unsafe abortion—less restrictive abortion laws and greater contraceptive use**—face social, religious, and political obstacles, particularly in developing nations, where most unsafe abortions (97%) occur. Even where these obstacles are overcome, women and health care providers need to be educated about contraception and the availability of legal and safe abortion, and women need better access to safe abortion and postabortion services. Otherwise, desperate women, facing the financial burdens and social stigma of unintended pregnancy and believing they have no other option, will continue to risk their lives by undergoing unsafe abortions.[108]

But even with unsafe abortion, 68,000 maternal deaths annually is less than

[107] WHO (World Health Organization). 2007. *Unsafe abortion: Global and Regional Estimates of the Incidence of Unsafe Abortion and Associated Mortality in 2003*. 5th ed. Geneva: World Health Organization. http://www.who.int/reproductivehealth/publications/unsafeabortion_2003/ua_estimates03.pdf. In Haddad, Lisa B., MD, MA. 2009. Unsafe Abortion: Unnecessary Maternal Mortality. Obstetrics and Gynecology. http://www.ncbi.nlm.nih.gov/pmc/articles/PMC2709326/

[108] ibid.; http://www.ncbi.nlm.nih.gov/pmc/articles/PMC2709326/

the 289,000 deaths[109] attributed to other "pregnancy or childbirth related causes."[110]

Pregnancy itself is risky, and physically costly (as is childcare/childrearing to majority), and the U.S. Supreme Court found that a woman has a right to privately make her own decision – autonomously in the first trimester -- about whether or not to take that risk with her body and to pay that price with the trajectory of her life.

And the cost to already-born women/girls of having no autonomy over their own lives and reproduction, or of being forced to seek unsafe, rather than safe, abortions is untenable.

As societies, we have a responsibility to protect those persons (and the civil rights and quality of life of those persons) who are already here – to not violate their civil rights or ignore their oppression for the sake of "potential" lives that might become – if the women/girls who didn't want to be pregnant in the first place are further oppressed by social structures (and/or partners) that pressure them to carry new lives – *that no one is waiting (with the resources or will) to care for* – to neonatal viability.

I know that when the Anti-Choice Movement argues for the gestating

---

[109] Even as the 289,000 deaths by "pregnancy or childbirth related causes" presumably include the 13% (or 68,000 women) who die annually of unsafe abortions (United Nations Population Fund)," there remain approximately 221,000 deaths per annum attributable to other pregnancy related causes, including: lack of access to obstetrical care, hemorrhage, infection, obstructed or prolonged labor without access to cesarean section, pregnancy-induced hypertension, preeclampsia, eclampsia, amniotic fluid embolism, pulmonary embolism, peripartum cardiomyopathy, intracranial hemorrhage, stroke, adolescent maternity, grand multiparity. WHO.Int, Nov 2015. Maternal Mortality: Fact Sheet #348. Media Centre. World Health Organization.
http://www.who.int/mediacentre/factsheets/fs348/en/)
[109] King, M.D., Jeffrey C. *Maternal Mortality in the United States: Current Status* (PowerPoint). ACOG.org. https://www.acog.org/-/media/Departments/Public-Health-and-Social-Issues/Maternal-Mortality-In-The-US.pdf?la=en
[110] United Nations Population Fund. [accessed] 20Aug 2016. *Maternal Health.* http://www.unfpa.org/maternal-health

lives of still unformed, unwanted, and unborn embryos, they do not step forward, en masse, to finance and parent them for the next 18 years (*or if disabled, to parent them for life and provide for them after parental death*). They do not see to it that each baby "saved" from abortion is clothed, and diapered, and fed, and loved, and educated, and brought up into a happy, balanced, productive, adulthood.

They do not (cannot) provide that which parents who are ready and wanting a child provide.

Instead, it is the girl/woman who didn't want/couldn't afford to be pregnant right then – or the State – that is expected to care for the children.

When you deny abortion, you do not make a wanted neonate or give a potential mother (financial/emotional/mental) resources. You do not fix relationships or marriages. You do not empower fathers to be more present or to make greater financial and emotional contributions to their offspring.

And most of the time, you do not secure, for that child, adoptive parents with sufficient resources, time, attention, and unconditional love. Instead, hundreds of thousands[111] of children wait for such parents in our foster care system.

And if the Anti-Choice Movement (of which I was once a part) were to succeed, and turn back Roe v. Wade, it is clear from the evidence (from our past, and from countries where abortion has been made illegal), that it would only return us to the days of back-alley abortions. It wouldn't change any individual girl or woman's circumstances in regard to any individual

---

[111] 400,000+ in care, 100,000 available for adoption. AEA (Adoption Exchange Association). (2002-2018). About the Children. AdoptUsKids.org.
https://www.adoptuskids.org/meet-the-children/children-in-foster-care/about-the-children

pregnancy.

Prohibiting abortion does not actually decrease abortion. It only increases the number of unsafe, illegal abortions.

Permitting abortion does not actually increase abortion. It only increases the number of safe abortions.

And even if we were to imagine that an army of willing, qualified, adoptive parents rose up to parent each unwanted embryo, "saved" from abortion[112] – no recompense would be made to the women and girls whose bodies/minds/and emotions were used – and permanently altered over the course of their pregnancies and deliveries – as they were forced to deal with the emotional aftermath of whatever situation made them desperate enough to seek an abortion in the first place, then forced them to carry to term, then forced them to deal with the repercussions of giving their newborn(s) away to strangers.

Women and girls are people, full human beings with complex lives/ needs/ dreams/ goals/ intellects/emotions/ and relationships – not baby-producing machines for boys and men – and not reproductive androids producing offspring as cheap labor for the nation state.

And so, in Roe v. Wade, the Supreme Court rightly honored that fact – the fact that it takes the resources of a full human being – a citizen with civil rights of her own -- with a reproductively-female human body – to produce another, viable, human body.

And that, even when the new being can breathe on its own, it takes

---

[112] At present, close to half a million children in the United States, sit in foster care, and about one hundred thousand are available for adoption, have no "permanent families" and sit, unadopted. . . .

long-term care (on average, two decades) before that newly-created human body can survive on its own (can feed itself/ clothe itself/ house itself/ keep itself safe/ educate itself/ and earn its own way in the world).

Roe v. Wade recognized the right to privacy of the girl/woman citizen to decide if she were willing to be so used and so engaged, for nine months – and then, for the next *eighteen+ years to life*.

Therefore, whatever one's theology, this secular, pluralist, democracy was founded on the idea that this nation-state cannot establish a religion – cannot mandate all citizens to follow one religion (even Christianity). Thus, the Court ruled that the potential life (the zygote → blastomer → morula → blastocyst → embryo → fetus) *does not have* a right to "be made" – *especially, in the first trimester* – and later, if there is a medical defect in the child, or a threat to the life of the potential-mother-to-be.

It ruled that women/girls have the right to choose whether – or not – to allow a pregnancy to progress in their bodies, and whether – or not – to have/raise a child. It ruled that the life of the *already-here, already-a-citizen, already autonomous* woman or girl among us has preeminence over the potential of an additional life, that cannot come into existence except she gestate and bear it.

I know that, to the evangelical mind, a female's right to privacy does not make sense.

One, women are believed to be created after Adam and for a different purpose. Their theology holds that Adam was created first to serve God, and that Eve was created later, and along with messing up and bringing sin into the world, she was created – not to serve God – but to serve Adam.

To evangelicals and fundamentalists, and to those who believe the doctrine of the Roman Catholic hierarchy, the zygote IS every bit *as alive* and of as much value, and demanding of as much protection, as the grown woman or teen girl – and thus, to save the equally-valuable life of the zygote/embryo, the impregnated female should be *forced to carry* (to term, if possible)

- To the fundamentalist religious mind, emergency contraception [which is not an abortifacient] and all forms of abortion, at all developmental stages, should be illegal and inaccessible – and whatever happens (as long as the women and girls cannot choose) will be God's will.

- To the fundamentalist religious mind, the woman's/girl's rights ended when she chose to cross the line from abstinence (or when it was crossed by force, in rape), and she should be made to go through whatever God has then ordained for her – in regard to both the impact of the pregnancy/childbirth/childrearing on her own health and life, and in regard to the health and life of the embryo.

- To the fundamentalist religious mind, even if the embryo is deformed, neither she nor her doctor should have any right to hurry the termination of the pregnancy or to shorten the duration of the lifespan of the seriously-ill fetus. If bringing the embryo/fetus to term will cause it to suffer – that is the will of God. If the woman or girl's life is ruined – that also is the will of God – and to be borne with as much grace as possible, for the sake of her own eternal soul.

But the United States is not a theocracy, and Christianity is not the state religion.

It is historical error to claim that the Founders intended the U.S. to be a Christian nation. In actuality, they founded a religiously pluralistic society in which everyone has the right to follow their own conscience, and the state does not have the right to "prohibit" the "free exercise" of religion – but neither may it impose (or "establish") any religion upon the populace at large.[113]

In the U.S., constitutionally, the theological belief in the ensoulment of the fertilized ovum (the zygote) is not enforceable, because it is a theological postulate – not a demonstrable scientific fact. To enforce that belief on those who do not hold it as their own religious belief, would be to "establish" a state religion in regard to a theological code about the "life" of the multi-staged early product of conception.

The Constitution is not the Bible, and science cannot establish the fertilized cell (in its early stages and where it cannot survive outside the womb) as sufficiently separate from its host to warrant it as a human being in possession of a civil right to life. It simply is not viable enough, even with advances in neonatal intensive care, to be separate until six months gestation or later.

So the Court ruled that the fertilized ovum does not have a "right to life."

The Court found, instead, that the owner of the hosting body – the girl/woman – has the right to decide whether – or not – to host the necessary process for the development of the potential inherent in the fertilized ovum.

However, the Court also ruled that, if a woman remains pregnant

---

[113] The pertinent clause of the First Amendment to the U.S. Constitution reads, "*Congress shall make no law respecting an establishment of religion, or prohibiting the free exercise thereof. . . .*" (Law.Cornell.edu. [accessed] 24 Aug 2016. *U.S. Constitution: First Amendment.* https://www.law.cornell.edu/constitution/first_amendment

through the first trimester, as a pregnancy progresses and the product of conception develops, her right to terminate her pregnancy legally decreases. The state has a "compelling interest" in the health of the woman through the second and third trimester, and a compelling interest in the product of conception (the potential life) once it becomes viable (i.e. attains enough development to be able to survive outside the womb, albeit, still with medical assistance).

It is, already, a matter of legal fact that *no woman* can simply walk in and get an abortion *at any time along the trajectory* of a pregnancy, just because she changes her mind.

Roe v. Wade NEVER gave any woman the right to terminate, without compelling medical complications, in the third trimester. And her rights to terminate are limited in the second trimester.

It has only ever been in the first trimester (before the embryo is a fetus - **0 to 13 Weeks**) that a woman can legally end a pregnancy "on demand."

The right to terminate a pregnancy, as stipulated by the U.S. Supreme Court in *Roe v. Wade, 410 U.S. 113* (1973) is only available on demand in the initial stages of a pregnancy. "In the first trimester" of a pregnancy, "the Court left the decision to abort completely to the woman and her physician."[114]

As stated, the Court made this ruling based on the girl's/woman's citizenship right to privacy:

> Justice Blackmun's majority opinion explicitly rejected a
> fetal "right to life" argument.[115] The Court instead

---

[114] *Roe v. Wade,* 410 U.S. at 163, https://en.wikipedia.org/wiki/Roe_v._Wade
[115] *Roe v. Wade*, 410 U.S. 113, Section IX (S. Ct. 1973).; See also Roe, 410 U.S. at 157–58

recognized the right to an abortion as a fundamental right included within the guarantee of personal privacy.[116]

While acknowledging that the right to abortion was not unlimited, Justice Blackmun, speaking for the Court, created a trimester framework **to balance the fundamental right** to abortion **with the government's two legitimate interests: protecting the mother's health and protecting the "potentiality of human life."** The trimester framework addressed when a woman's fundamental right to abortion would be absolute [the first trimester], and when the state's interests would become compelling. In the first trimester . . . the Court left the decision to abort completely to the woman and her physician.[117] From approximately the end of the first trimester until fetal viability, the state's interest in protecting the health of the mother would become "compelling."[118]

Therefore, abortions done in the second trimester (14 to 26 Weeks) are not on demand by the woman, but are generally only done with a doctor's approval, and then, only because there is a serious medical issue for the developing fetus and/or for the health or medical survival of the mother. "From approximately the end of the first trimester until fetal viability,[119] the

---

[116] *Roe v. Wade,* 410 U.S at 153 "This right of privacy, whether it be founded in the Fourteenth Amendment's concept of personal liberty and restrictions upon state action, as we feel it is, or, as the District Court determined, in the Ninth Amendment's reservation of rights to the people, is broad enough to encompass a woman's decision whether or not to terminate her pregnancy." (emphasis mine) https://en.wikipedia.org/wiki/Roe_v._Wade
[117] *Roe v. Wade,* 410 U.S at 163
[118] See *id.* at 163
[119] Again, if set at when most newborns would be able to live on their own outside the womb without medical assistance, fetal viability would be set at about the 8th month. Today, fetal viability is set at the gestational weeks in which a fetus can be reasonably expected to survive with *intensive* medical intervention.

state's interest in protecting the health of the mother" is viewed as "compelling,"[120] therefore, the Court continued to allow abortion in the second trimester, but only for medical reasons – so the physician must find that either the health or life of the girl/woman would be endangered by carrying the fetus to viability, or the physician must find serious disease of the fetus, before a second trimester pregnancy can be legally terminated.[121]

> The Court ruled 7–2 that a right to privacy under the Due Process Clause of the 14th Amendment extended to a woman's decision to have an abortion, but that this right must be balanced against the state's two legitimate interests in regulating abortions: protecting women's health and protecting the potentiality of human life.[122] Arguing that these **state interests became stronger over the course of a pregnancy**, the Court resolved this balancing test by **tying state regulation of abortion to the third trimester of pregnancy**.[123]

In the third trimester (27 to 40 Weeks), or at fetal viability,[124] "the state's interest in the "potential life" (of the now-viable-with-medical-assistance fetus) is viewed as "compelling, and the state can regulate abortion to protect that "potential life.""[125] At that point (the third trimester), the state can even forbid abortion so long as it makes an exception to preserve the life or health of the mother"[126] – which is to say that in the third trimester

---

[120] See *id.* at 163, https://en.wikipedia.org/wiki/Roe_v._Wade

[121] *Roe v. Wade,* https://en.wikipedia.org/wiki/Roe_v._Wade

[122] *Roe v. Wade*, 410 U.S. 113, 162 ("We repeat, however, that the State does have an important and legitimate interest in preserving and protecting the health of the pregnant woman, whether she be a resident of the State or a non-resident who seeks medical consultation and treatment there, and that it has still another important and legitimate interest in protecting the potentiality of human life.")

[123] *Roe v. Wade,* 410 U.S. https://en.wikipedia.org/wiki/Roe_v._Wade

[124] Formerly at about 26 weeks, now, since the practice of neonatal intensive care has improved [with limited chance of survival] at about 23 to 24 weeks. *Planned Parenthood v. Casey*, 505 U.S. at 860. (1992), https://en.wikipedia.org/wiki/Roe_v._Wade

[125] See *id.* at 163, https://en.wikipedia.org/wiki/Roe_v._Wade

[126] *Id.* at 163–64 ("If the State is interested in protecting fetal life after viability, it may go so

(or after 23-24 weeks), the only abortion that is legal is one of absolute medical necessity. Whether or not a woman could access a third trimester abortion illegally, accessing a third trimester abortion legally is a rare exception (it is also, comparatively, far more expensive) – and done only for compelling medical reasons. The state has claimed a compelling interest in protecting the life of a late-term fetus that could, with neonatal intensive care intervention, survive outside of the womb.

Generally, if a woman has regular periods, and thus, realizes she is pregnant early in the gestational process, and if she has the means (generally financial), and if she has access (if there are facilities within non-stressful/economically-viable geographic reach), and if she knows her own mind about a given pregnancy, and if abortion is her choice, she will not put the procedure off.

The earlier a woman seeks an abortion, the easier it is to obtain, the easier it is on her body, and the less it is likely to cost. If she acts quickly enough, she may even be able to abort medically (through pills), rather than surgically.

However, sometimes a woman wants very much to be pregnant, then finds that the fetus she is carrying will not become viable and/or will suffer greatly if born. Some of the tests that determine genetic diseases cannot be

---

far as to proscribe [forbid] abortion during that period, except when it is necessary to preserve the life or health of the mother."), https://en.wikipedia.org/wiki/Roe_v._Wade

administered until the mid-second trimester or later.[127]

Patients coming in for very late abortion - over 26 menstrual weeks' gestation - are almost always seeking services for termination of a **desired pregnancy** that has developed serious complications. This usually means the discovery of a catastrophic fetal anomaly or genetic disorder that guarantees death, suffering, or serious disability for the baby that would be delivered if the pregnancy were to continue to term.

In these cases, Roe v. Wade intended to allow the patient and her doctor to proceed.

As stated before, in the case where a fetus has reached viability, and the mother's life is in jeopardy, the fetus would be delivered early by Cesarean section, and treated in neonatal intensive care, in the hope that both mother and child will survive.

---

[127] Hern, Warren, M.D., M.P.H., Ph.D. Third Trimester Abortion. http://www.drhern.com/en/abortion-services/third-trimester-abortion.html; "I had a 2nd trimester abortion at 18 weeks and 3 days pregnant. I was not involved in rape or incest. I was not an unwed teenager. I did not have financial concerns with raising another child. I was not using abortion as a form of birth control. My baby was not unloved, unwanted, an accident or a mistake. My situation is rarely talked about, but it should be." 1in3 Campaign.org. [accessed] 24 Aug 2016. *Hadleigh. http://www.1in3campaign.org/written-stories/4030#more-4030*

~~~

You *Already Are* a Mother

A Narrative

As Tony rounded the corner, and steered us straight into a immovable wall of spitting protestors, I struggled to breathe.

I turned my face away from their Photoshopped images of grisly fetal remains, labeled as 1st term, while clearly 3rd. I had already, just two days before, been forced to watch an ultrasound of my own 8 ½ week embryo, and I knew that it wasn't formed like the ketchup-spattered fabrications on their placards. It didn't have tiny finger and toes – only buds where hands and feet might develop. It looked more like a tadpole than a human. I'd seen. They had made me look.

Also, because of state law, the doctor had been required to make me listen to the fetal "heart" beat, but I knew from the gestational stages I'd looked up, that there actually wasn't a heart in there yet – just the pulse of an early vein that had begun its rhythm well in advance of the formation of a recognizable organ.

It was already such a somber day, I couldn't bear their exaggerations. I wanted to cry , to scream, because they were invading my well-thought out space.

The weight of the air on my chest felt like a dentist's lead apron.

This wasn't supposed to be happening. I was supposed to be impregnable! It had been 11 years since my endometrial ablation, and I hadn't gotten pregnant, lo, those 11 years. It simply wasn't supposed to be possible.

My heavy periods had been so severe that, once I had my children – my boy and my girl – I had pestered my doctor for an ablation, to alter the walls of my uterus and stop my flow. No more pain. No more flooding. But my ovaries were left intact, so I wasn't slammed – at 33 – into premature menopause. I didn't lose my sex drive. My skin didn't grow suddenly thin and crêpe-y. I was still a young woman – just a young woman who already had all the children she wanted, and who no longer had severe, period-induced, anemia and monthly bouts of agony – which was, quite frankly, pure bliss.

And then the divorce had come.

He had left me – a single mom – and I was grateful at an even deeper level for the ablation – grateful not to be a single parent of three or four, instead of two.

And then, I had gotten another surgery. My weight had been out of control, so I sought out weight loss surgery, and lucked into the Cadillac of procedures – a Duodenal Switch[128] – that reduced the capacity of my stomach *and* rerouted my digestive track – restriction and mal-absorption in one – and the weight had melted away – and stayed off – and Tony had danced into my (now) skinny life, and we had fallen madly, deeply, passionately in love.

And we made a great blended family – each of us with children that generally got along, and we had merged our lives and our homes, and made wonderful, regular use of my inability to get pregnant.

The idea was that a fertilized ovum could not implant into an ablated uterus, because there was no endometrial lining to sustain it.

So I was more stunned than scared. I may even have been in shock.

My gynecologist, and another gynecologist we sought out for a second opinion, laid it out in no uncertain terms.

If I attempted to carry this pregnancy, well before I got

---

[128] A biliopancreatic diversion with duodenal switch

anywhere near fetal viability, I would be dead. Echoing each other, they let us know that – even though some small portion of my uterine wall had allowed implantation – enough of the lining had been scarred by the ablation that, if I attempted to carry, as my uterus expanded, it would explode. Not unlike an ectopic pregnancy, the growth of the embryo would kill me. I could not carry long enough to deliver.

And there were the children I already had, ages 7 and 11. They needed me. They needed me to live. And my stepchildren, Tony's 8 and 12 year old, with whom I had bonded.

The sea of protestors surrounded our car and beat on the windows. *"Drive to the right,"* I groaned toward Tony. *"The clinic said the parking is on the right."* I fumbled with my phone, struggling with the number I'd preset to text the clinic escorts.

Two women in florescent vests emerged from the clinic entrance, marched past the protestors lined up behind the barricade tape that demarcated the buffer zone, and met us at our car. Ever the law-abiding Christians (the protestors) fell back at their approach, but the protestors' words crossed all police tape and distance – *"Don't kill your baby!" We'll help. Talk to us. You have options. Jesus doesn't want you to do this. You already are a mother!"*

"Damn right, I am," I thought, *"and my children need me to survive this contraceptive failure!"*

"You don't know me! You don't know what I'm going through!" I yelled back, but the strong arms of the woman on my right, and Tony on my left, guided me past their wild eyes, through the bullet-proof glass doors, and into the inner sanctum.

Before we could move forward, we had to do it again. Another ultrasound. And again, I had to view still photos of the uterine mass. And sign my consent – again.

I quietly gave thanks that I was not underage. In my state, minors had to get parental consent. I had read the statistics on early teen girls impregnated by family members, even their own fathers, then forced to seek their perpetrator's signature – or demand a hearing with a judge to explain to (*most likely*) "him" the shame of the incest that caused them to seek his dispensation from the parental consent law.

Tears rolled silently down my face during the ultrasound. I lay there, looking at Tony's chiseled features, and suddenly wanted so much to have this baby – his baby!

If only I *could* carry it, *Would it have his eyes? that little cleft in his chin?*

It would be hard to start over again. My youngest would be 8 and a half by the time *he? she?* was born. But I loved Tony enough, if there were a choice, I might have made the other one, just this once.

But ultrasound or not, pulsing vein beating promise of things to come, or not, my uterus simply couldn't do it.

I set my un-cleft chin to what had to be, and signed my consent. My living children needed me. My living, breathing man wanted me. I wanted me – here, and whole – and not exploded.

State stipulations finally behind us, they escorted Tony back to the waiting room, and rolled me into treatment. Everything got better as soon as they started to administer the nitrous oxide. That which had been full of blockades – mandatory ultrasounds and embryonic "heart"beats, frothing mobs, gynecologists who couldn't explain why the ablation had been insufficient – melted into warmth and kindness. I noticed how concerned the staff was with my well-being. A nurse held my hand and asked how I was doing. The doctor down between my legs, explained each step in detail before making her next move. They double-checked a final time, *Was I sure this was my decision?*

I didn't feel the dilation of my cervix. Floating in my laughing gas, I was flooded with gratitude for the peace and safety of that space. When they rolled me from treatment to recovery, they let Tony in, and I looked up, sighing gratitude for the love in his eyes looking back at me. Each step, he had been there for me. He sat with me, fingers entwining mine, as I let the drugs wear off. Then he helped me dress, gathered my discharge instructions, and brought the car around as the escorts pushed me out – and into the mob again.

A woman with a full twin stroller and a toddler in arms shouted prayers for me, asking her god to *"forgive* me *for killing my baby."* A great-grandmother rolled her prayer beads in her hand, loudly reciting, *"Hail Mary, full of grace, the Lord is with thee,"* as the escorts helped Tony help me back into the passenger seat.

Back home, I crawled into bed and curled up, emotionally exhausted from the ordeal. It was not the hygienic office, the sterile operating room, or the sufficient pain management that got me. It was the state regulations – the double ultrasounds, the embryonic pulse played to a woman who'd had two successful, planned, pregnancies – and the terror of the mob that waylaid us on the way in – and again, on the way out – all meant to reduce, or at least complicate, my ability to choose what was best for myself – and my already existing family.

With a single bathroom break, I slept twenty-hours straight.

The next day, Tony let them in, breakfast tray in hand, at noon.

There was a poached egg, and toast, and a small Ball jar of orange juice, and a single white rose. My 7-year-old beamed as she described how Tony taught her how to poach the egg, and the 11-year-old talked up the way he buttered the toast – not too much, but not too little – just the way he knows I like it. Climbing into bed on either side of me, they squabbled about which movie to watch, as my smile widened. Tony topped the night off with his signature foot massage.

When I returned to my Ob/Gyn, he wouldn't give me birth control, insisting that the failure of the ablation was a contraindication to hormonal contraceptives. He pressed me to do a tubal ligation or a uterine hysterectomy.

I insisted, I simply needed to be sure I didn't end up pregnant again, that (even though it had partially failed) with the fact of the ablation, I didn't see the need for a tubal or a hysterectomy.

I noticed an orange sticker in my chart. When he turned in his chair, I could read it. The sticker said, "Abortion."

He had, quite literally, labeled me.

I changed doctors.

For a time, I went on the birth control implant, Implanon. Eventually, Tony got a vasectomy. It became such an obvious way to control our fertility.

I shudder when I think, if I not been able to access my abortion safely and legally, I would have had to access one illegally – because my life was actually at risk.

And I am grateful to be here, to not have left my already-born children, orphaned.

I was – already – a mother.

~~~

9. HISTORICAL BACKGROUND

A little background history of the abortion issue is imperative. As a people, we must know our collective history in order to make decisions for our present and our future. **We cannot know where we are, or where we should go, if we do not know where we have come from.** That history shows that, **"expanding access to contraception, rather than restricting abortion, will ultimately save women's lives."**[129]

Justice Blackmun researched the issue before issuing his ruling.

> According to the Court, "the restrictive criminal abortion laws in effect in a majority of States today are of relatively recent vintage." Providing a historical analysis on abortion, Justice Harry Blackmun noted that abortion was "resorted to without scruple" in Greek and Roman times.[130] Blackmun also addressed the permissive and restrictive abortion attitudes and laws throughout history, noting the disagreements among leaders (of all different professions) in those eras and the formative laws and cases.[131] In the United States, in 1821, Connecticut passed the first state statute criminalizing abortion [so abortion was legal in the United States until 1821, when, as medicine professionalized and licensure was mandated and only

---

[129] Think Progess.org. 4Oct 2012. *47,000 Women Die Each Year From Unsafe Abortions.* https://thinkprogress.org/47-000-women-die-each-year-from-unsafe-abortions-d20eae29f11c#.8p3kqj1sj
[130] *Roe v. Wade*, 410 U.S. at 130
[131] *Roe v. Wade*, 410 U.S. at 131–36, 143

available to males, laws began to be passed to take access away]. Every state had abortion legislation by 1900.[132] . . . Justice Blackmun would conclude that the criminalization of abortion did not[133] have "roots in the English common-law tradition."[134] . . . In his opinion, Blackmun also clearly explained how he had reached the trimester framework – scrutinizing history, common law, the Hippocratic Oath, medical knowledge, and the positions of medical organizations.[135]

In all times and eras, women (who did not want to be pregnant) of all ages (from menses to menopause), of all races and ethnicities, and of all spiritual or religious backgrounds, have:

- first – been driven to (where desirable and possible) prevent conception, and

- second – where contraception was not available (or failed), to access abortion.

Legal or illegal, within each category of woman, approximately the same proportion have sought, and continue to seek, abortions.

Overall, today, a large percentage of American women – somewhere

---

[132] "*By 1900 every state in the Union had an anti-abortion prohibition.*" Cole, George & Stanislaw Frankowski. 1987. Abortion and Protection of the Human Fetus: Legal Problems in a Cross-Cultural Perspective. Martinus Nijhoff Publishers. (p.20).
[133] Greenhouse, Linda 2005. *Becoming Justice Blackmun: Harry Blackmun's Supreme Court Journey.* New York: Times Books. (p. 92)
[134] https://en.wikipedia.org/wiki/Roe_v._Wade
[135] *See Roe v. Wade*, 410 U.S. at 129–47, https://en.wikipedia.org/wiki/Roe_v._Wade

between 27%[136] and 43%[137] -- access their right to legal abortion at least once in their reproductive lives (between menses and menopause). And they do so as early in an unwanted pregnancy as is possible for them, in their given circumstances, and with their given knowledge and resources.

Where abortion is not an option, throughout human history, infanticide

---

[136] "While claiming that it is a "Myth that 1 in 3 women have abortions" anti-choice proponents still claim that "27.9%" ("not 33%") of "U.S. women will have an abortion between age 15 and 44." Enriquez, Lauren. 28 Nov 2014. *Myth that 1 in 3 Women Have Abortions Persists Despite Hard Evidence to the Contrary.* LiveActionNews.org. http://liveactionnews.org/myth-that-1-in-3-women-have-abortions-persists-despite-hard-evidence-to-the-contrary/; "30 percent of women (effectively, one in three) will have an abortion by age 45, *if the 2008 abortion rate prevailed. . . .* But . . . the abortion rate for women ages 15 to 44 dropped by 13 percent between 2008 and 2011. Rachel Jones, Guttmacher Institute's principal research scientist who conducted the abortion rate and lifetime incidence studies, said it's "quite possible" that the "one in three" statistic has changed because of the decline in abortion rate since 2008. (Studies show the abortion rate declined further between 2011 and 2013.) But it's impossible to predict whether the lifetime incidence statistic would increase or decrease, because it depends on how the number of women having first-time abortions changed during that period. Guttmacher Institute is now analyzing 2014 Abortion Patient Survey results from more than 8,000 women. This survey is done every six to eight years, and this is the first update since 2008. An updated figure for the "one in three" lifetime incidence will not be available until early 2017. . . . Intuitively, we would [expect to] see a decline . . . based on past patterns. But again, it's a little more complicated than that. . . . In 2008, about half of abortion patients had had their first abortion (more than half of women ages 25 and older had had an abortion). If fewer women who had abortions in 2014 have had a prior abortion, this could potentially result in a higher lifetime incidence, Jones said. Teen birth, teen pregnancy and teen abortion rates also have declined since 2008. If most of the abortion rate decline is due substantially to declining teen abortions, it may not have much effect on the overall lifetime incidence, Jones said. If large numbers of teens had abortions after they aged out of the 15-19 range, the lifetime incidence would not change by much. *Among the potential reasons for the abortion rate decline is that more women are using highly effective contraceptive methods, like intrauterine devices (IUDs) that are implanted and decrease the risk of user error. In recent years, some states imposed new restrictions on abortions. Plus, the Affordable Care Act went into effect in January 2014, expanding women's access to preventive care (including contraception). (emphasis mine).* Lee, Michelle Ye Hee. 30 Sep 2015. *The Stale Claim That 'One In Three' Women Will Have An Abortion By Age 45.* https://www.washingtonpost.com/news/fact-checker/wp/2015/09/30/the-stale-claim-that-one-in-three-women-will-have-an-abortion-by-age-45/

[137] "Almost half of American women (43 percent) will have an abortion sometime in their lifetime." FoxNews.com. 17 June 2003. *Fast Facts: U.S. Abortion Statistics.* http://www.foxnews.com/story/2003/06/17/fast-facts-us-abortion-statistics.html; "At 2008 abortion rates, almost one in 10 women will have an abortion by age 20, one in four by age 30 and **three in 10 by age 45.**" Guttmacher Institute. May 2016. *Induced Abortion in the United States.* https://www.guttmacher.org/fact-sheet/induced-abortion-united-states

(the murder of full-term babies at, or just after, birth) – a far less desirable option – has been (and is still) practiced.[138] Infanticide (particularly of female newborns) was, and is, common – wherever people cannot prevent conception (or, given gender bias, cannot prevent the birth of girl neonates). Across time and culture, even poor and struggling parents have been highly unlikely to commit infanticide against male neonates, as they are considered a financial advantage [when grown], even as girl children are considered a financial liability across their lifespans [a burden to feed/bringing in no money and being given/sold away as labor to another family when grown]).

In the U.S., when abortion was illegal, the same approximate proportion of women – at great risk to themselves – still accessed unsafe, back-alley abortions. At the time of the Roe v. Wade ruling, thousands of women died each year from the work of unskilled and unsafe practitioners.[139]

> Because many deaths were not officially attributed to unsafe, illegal abortion, it's impossible to know the exact number of lives lost. However, *thousands of women a year* were treated for health complications due to botched, unsanitary, or self-induced abortions, and many died. Others were left infertile or with chronic illness and pain.[140]

Proportional to the population, and based on what we know of nations where abortion is illegal today, in the U.S., this appears to have been true from Colonial times to the present. Women who access abortion are both

---

[138] See film, Davis, Evan Grae. (dir.). 2012. *"It's a Girl."* Shadowline Films.
[139] Our Bodies Our Selves. 28 Mar 2014/18 May 2016. *History of Abortion in the U.S.* http://www.ourbodiesourselves.org/health-info/u-s-abortion-history
[140] ibid

single and married, range in age from puberty to menopause, and were/are – in about equal proportions – from all religious (and non-religious) belief systems. There are situations that, for the woman who has found herself pregnant, are simply untenable.

Access to legal, safe, abortion helps protect the lives of women and girls.

Making abortion illegal, risks the lives of the same proportion of women and girls whose lives were/are protected by legal abortion.

As a spiritual/religious person, I do *not* know when the "soul" enters the body – whether the soul enters at the zygote stage, or the blastomer, or the morula, or the blastocyst, or the embryo,[141] or waits to enter until "quickening" (when the mother can feel the developing fetus[142] moving

---

[141] "Whether the embryo is a human person at this state of development is a hotly contested debate. Most in the [anti-choice] community say that it has been a person since conception. They often refer to pre-embryos and embryos as "babies." Most in the pro-choice community refer to it as an embryo and believe that personhood is only attained much later in gestation -- perhaps at birth. This lack of agreement generates most of the conflict, heat, and anger over women's abortion access." http://www.religioustolerance.org/abo_fetu.htm

[142] "**3 weeks**: The embryo is now about 1/12" long, the size of a pencil point. It most closely resembles a worm - long and thin and with a segmented end. Its heart begins to beat about 18 to 21 days after conception. Before this time, the woman might have noticed that her menstrual period is late; she might suspect that she is pregnant and conduct a pregnancy test. In the U.S., about half of all pregnancies are unplanned. About half of these are terminated by an abortion. **4 weeks:** The embryo is now about 1/5" long. It looks something like a tadpole. The structure that will develop into a head is visible, as is a noticeable tail. The embryo has structures like the gills of a fish in the area that will later develop into a throat. **5 weeks:** Tiny arm and leg buds have formed. Hands with webs between the fingers have formed at the end of the arm buds. Fingerprints are detectable. The face *"has a distinctly reptilian aspect . . . the embryo still has a tail and cannot be distinguished from pig, rabbit, elephant, or chick embryo* [at this stage of development]." **6 weeks:** The embryo is about 1/2" long. The face has two eyes, one on each side of its head. The front of the face has *"connected slits where the mouth and nose eventually will be."* **7 weeks:** The embryo has almost lost its tail. *"The face is mammalian but somewhat pig-like."* Pain sensors appear. Many religious and social conservatives believe that the embryo at this stage can feel pain. However, the higher functions of the brain have yet to develop, and the pathways to transfer pain signals from the pain sensors to the brain do not exist at this stage of development." http://www.religioustolerance.org/stages-of-human-embryo-and-fetal-debelopment.htm.

around inside her (likely to first occur midway through the second trimester), or enters the fetus during the potentially-viable third trimester, or enters the neonate just prior to or during birth, or waits to enter until the newborn infant inhales the first "breath of life."

No one actually knows. The only Scripture verse that comes to mind is in Genesis 2:7, where Adam came to life as God breathed into "him" the "breath of life." In Psalm 139:15, when the Psalmist was told that he was "fearfully and wonderfully made" "in secret" in his mothers' womb, with his "substance" not "hidden" from God, he may simply have been talking about the development of the body. Even for the religiously-minded, it does not actually provide "scriptural evidence" of when the soul enters.

To the one who believes the soul enters as the ovum is fertilized (the creation of the zygote, the two-celled fertilized ovum) there is no question that any method or device that might keep a zygote from implanting in the uterine wall, is an instrument of murder.

*NOTE: According to researchers, neither the birth control pill, nor emergency contraception [the morning after pill], are abortifacients. They do not cast off the product of conception, but as hormonal methods, **they** both **prevent ovulation**[143] in the first place).[144]

---

[143] 'If the woman has not ovulated recently, has unprotected sexual intercourse, wants to avoid a pregnancy, and takes a morning after pill quickly, it will normally prevent ovulation. If ovulation has already occurred, it will normally prevent conception. If conception has already occurred, medical researchers have determined that the pill will have no effect. However, many religious, social, and political conservatives have chosen to ignore the findings of the researchers, and assert – without proof – that the morning after pill (a.k.a. emergency contraception) can prevent implantation in the inner wall of the uterus." http://www.religioustolerance.org/abo_fetu.htm

[144] "Medical researchers once speculated If the woman has taken emergency contraception (a.k.a. EC & the "morning after" pill) quickly after unprotected intercourse, *and* it has not prevented ovulation, *and* it has not prevented conception, then the EC might prevent the blastocyst from attaching to the wall of the womb. However, further **research has shown** that this third mechanism appears to be impossible. That is, EC acts as a true contraceptive.

Yet, science would argue that human consciousness cannot exist before the human brain has developed,[145] and the brain is not developed enough to experience consciousness, to become sentient, until at or about viability (until about 26 weeks) . . . . It is known that in the first trimester, the embryonic brain is developing, but has not yet developed.[146]

Many anti-choice groups and religious conservatives reject the research findings and still assume that the EC can prevent implantation. Since these groups generally regard pregnancy as having been started at conception, they regard emergency contraception as a possible abortifacient. Many routinely refer to it as an actual abortifacient. In spite of manufacturers' objections, and the findings of research scientists, the U.S. federal government still requires EC packaging to state that preventing implantation is still a possibility."
http://www.religioustolerance.org/abo_fetu.htm

[145] "Many religious progressives and secularists note that if a soul exists it cannot function until about the 26th week of pregnancy, after the fetus becomes sentient. Only then do its higher brain functions first appear, and the fetus becomes aware of its environment to some degree." http://www.religioustolerance.org/abo_fetu.htm

[146] **2 months:** The embryo's face resembles that of a primate but is not fully human in appearance. Some of the brain begins to form; this is the primitive "*reptilian brain*" that will function throughout life. The embryo will respond to prodding, although it has no consciousness at this stage of development. The brain's higher functions are not active until much later in pregnancy when the fetus becomes sentient. . . . **10 weeks:** The embryo is now called a fetus. Its face looks human. Its genetic gender may be predicted from the presence or absence of a penis during an ultrasound test. **13 weeks or 3 months:** The fetus is about 3 inches long and weighs about an ounce. Fingernails and bones can be seen. Over 90% of all abortions are performed before this stage, before the fetus has become conscious, and therefore before it is sentient. http://www.religioustolerance.org/stages-of-human-embryo-and-fetal-debelopment.htm.

~ ~ ~

Not a Kitten

A Narrative

It was exciting, being in Dan's arms. Exciting enough to make me sneak down the uncarpeted, creaky, 100-year-old, wooden steps from my bedroom on the third floor, past my parents' bedroom on the second, to the first, and out the back door, to meet him in an unlocked car down the block. I loved the feel of his kisses on my neck, and the look in his eyes – like I was the most beautiful thing he'd ever seen.

He kept wanting me to go further and further. All the kids in the neighborhood were starting to go further. In the Quinlan's garage, a lot of sex and near-sex was played out each weekend. When we got locked out, we were told some of the older boys and girls were *"going all the way."* When we were let in, there were long *make-out* sessions, with kids pairing up and hiding in different corners – one couple making out on the cement floor behind the motorbike, and another making out in the seat of the lawn tractor, and another stretched out beneath Mr. Quinlan's workbench.

I only wanted to make-out with Dan. He was soooo cool.

He was tall, with broad shoulders, on which hung a chestnut brown, fringed, suede jacket that wrapped me in the warmth of its smell, and the strength of his arms, whenever I curled into it – and made me feel like nothing in the whole world could hurt me. Being with him made me feel grown up.

I loved his dark hair that curled down over his shoulders, and his black eyes that flashed with intelligence as he expounded on the evils of *"The System"* – and how we all needed to resist that System by crafting alternative lives. *"Who needs money?"* Dan would pontificate, suggesting we *"could live in the forest, in harmony with nature, out in a National Park"* where the boys could throw together campsites *"of brush and hides"* and *"hunt small game,"* while the girls studied *"which wild plants were good as edibles."*

Or he and I could *"thumb it to California to live on the beach."* I could *"waitress,"* while he *"made connections and got into a band."*

It all sounded lovely, even the waitressing or learning to eat small game, because it all included him, and his kisses, and his sparkling black eyes, and being grown, and away from my parents and the restrictions of adolescence.

So I snuck out, night after night, and met him in an unlocked car, and little by little, I went further. He wanted to go *"all the way,"* and part of me thought, *"No, I shouldn't. I don't want to get pregnant right now."* And part of me thought, *"Yes, I should. Even if I got pregnant right now, a baby would be the beginning of our life together, and he would make such a beautiful baby, if it had his dark eyes."*

So I let him. One night, I just let him. And then another night. And another.

It felt close and warm, to have him inside me. And I had never felt so loved. It made up for all the kids in school who hadn't really liked me, and for the fights with my mother, who always said, *"No,"* when I needed a *"Yes."* It felt like coming home after a long separation.

Then I began to throw up, and my period didn't come. And when I told him, he said this was, *"our chance."* Now, we *"had to strike out."* We would *"head to California,"* and I would waitress, and he would watch the kid till I got home, then *"play nights in a band,"* and get *"famous,"* and we'd have *"more than enough."*

So we picked the day of the week, and instead of heading for school, I boarded a bus to Center City and we met at the main terminal. We headed for D.C., then stuck out our thumbs for California.

We had no money. And the South was an odd place to signal for rides as a teenage girl, in a multicolored poncho, and a long-haired hippie. I was still early enough not to show, so we got rides easily. Most of our drivers offered us a beer, or a hit on their joint, and let us off at the next town.

But hitchhiking across the country, three months pregnant, was dusty, and exhausting, and my frequent need to pee was one of our biggest problems. When I couldn't hold it, we'd lose our ride. Few who picked us up were willing to delay their trips for my pregnant bladder.

And in some states, nature was unforgiving. There were fire ants and poisonous snakes and mosquitoes the size of dragonflies. And if no better offers came, at nights, we were forced to creep off the highway, relieved ourselves in a stand of brush, pull some bologna, cheese, and Wonder Bread from my backpack, and lean back against a tree – taking turns sleeping – so one of us was always on guard.

The trucker who picked us up on the last stretch into Kansas City offered us a shower in his motel room. It had been days and days since I'd gotten to wash up or change clothes. It felt like a gift from God. Dan didn't believe in God. Secure in his intellectual superiority, he thought it superstitious to hold *"magical thinking"* in the *"myth"* of *"an imaginary Sky God"* – letting me know that *"really smart"* people only believed in what they can prove through the scientific method.

Nevertheless, I was ecstatic about the opportunity to feel the rush of warm water on my scalp and back, washing the dirt away in a shower of fresh suds. As I stepped into the shower, I let out a small squeal of joy and breathed a moment's gratitude.

I was busy enjoying the feeling of being clean, when a hand clamped over my mouth and an arm slipped around my melon-shaped waist, pulling me backward from the tub. Biting and kicking, I found myself tossed onto the burnt orange and rust brown bedspread, and mounted by the now-naked trucker. Craning my neck, I saw Dan, gagged and bound to the second bed. The trucker's blond beard scratched my face and as he rushed to his climax, then collapsed, panting on top of me.

After a few moments, he abruptly stood up, gathered my clothes, and commanded me to dress. Retrieving a handgun from his own clothing, he pointed it at Dan and I, barking orders on how to release him, then put us out on the street – threatening that if we told anyone, or went to the police, he would say we tried to rob him. He reminded us, that as "*runaways*," there was "*surely*" an "*All-Points Bulletin*" out for "*our capture*", and our "*juvenile delinquent*" word would never hold up against "*his*" word, as a "*law-abiding adult.*"

In the woods behind the motel, I broke down, disjointed by the transition from the glory of that shower to such abject filth. I had never felt so dirty. . . so used. . . so vulnerable. . . so unable to protect the integrity of my own body   so defiled

Weary and hungry – and needing a clean that a thousand showers could never return – wordlessly – we turned and began to hitchhike home. We simply headed East.

About a day into our return, I spotted a stream, and climbed down the bank just to stand in it, and to let its water rush through my clothing and across my skin. Tears washed my cheeks, as Dan hung his head. When threatened with death, he had submitted. He had watched, helplessly, as the girl he loved was raped. He sagged under his failure, his inability to protect the integrity of my body, a body that he loved, or to protect our developing connection, growing inside me. We had all been at the perpetrator's mercy.

When we arrived home, his mother welcomed him with warmth, relieved at her son's return, not angry at the news of a potential grandchild.

When we arrived home, my parents barred the door, letting me in – only – upon a list of conditions.

My return was not a source of joy. After the initial terror that I had been kidnapped, they remembered my vomiting. In my absence, their anger had grown. My unwed pregnancy brought shame to their standing in our community. To bring me back *"into line with The Faith," "as long as I lived under their roof,"* there would be no more *"fornication."* They would begin arrangements for an *in-faith* adoption, and I could see Dan, only, with a chaperone.

I told them Dan and I wanted our baby, and that I would live with him as soon as he got a job and a place. He did not believe in marriage, would not make me *"right"* in the eyes of *"The Church."* He did not believe in the right of church, or state, to issue a fiat to validate our love. But he did love me and would help me raise our child.

Under duress, I was forced to agree to their terms, until Dan could save me from them. Dan could not come into their home, and I must submit to their chaperoning when I went out. I must return to school and keep my grades up. And when the baby was born, if I would not sign it away, I must get a job, and find and pay for daycare while at work and at school. They would not pay for a sitter – or babysit.

The lockdown was hard. I missed not being with Dan 24/7. Except for Kansas City, I missed traveling with him, missed sleeping in his arms, missed his passion – missed his kiss.

A few times I snuck out – without an older-sibling-chaperone – but the bigger my belly grew, the harder it was to traverse the creaky stairs late at night.

So I poured my attention into dreaming about the job he would find and the apartment he would rent, and into studying the stages of gestation. Week by week, I charted the body parts my fetus was developing. And, since there were no ultrasounds then to reveal the gender, I began to crochet infant outfits in lemon- and lime- colored yarns.

One morning, desperate to see him unattended, I cut school.

I wanted a warm place to sit and talk. I needed to know what we were doing, in little less than a month. But there was no inside place where we might not be seen by someone, anyone, who knew my parents.

I met him – past the center of town – behind the train station – where a long row of blue spruce ran the length of exposed track, offering privacy. Summer and fall had turned into the depths of winter, and I was heavy with my eighth month. The day was a brisk, but sunlit, 20 degrees, and the snow lay a foot deep, and frozen over, with little puddles of ice-melt where the sun broke through the branches.

Dan began to press for intimacy. I wanted to be close to him, too. It had been a long time, and I wanted to relax into the knowing that he would come through, that everything would be all right. . . .

He was having trouble finding a way for us to move in together. He hadn't found a job. After all, he (suddenly) *"had plans for college,"* and without, *"at least, his high school diploma,"* work options were *"bleak."* And his mother wouldn't take me in. She couldn't afford to support two more mouths.

He began to press harder for sex, but being daytime, there was little chance of crawling into the warmth and privacy of the back of an unlocked vehicle.

He began to pressure me to lie down in the icy snow, so he could just get it in and get off. His dark eyes flashed – with anger and disdain. He was *"horny,"* and *"IF I loved him,"* I would meet his needs, *"now."* It had been *"a long time. . . ."*

I felt my heart break.

Confused, I tried to accommodate. I did my best to lie down in the snow, but the puddles of water the sun had melted, penetrated my insufficient cloth coat – and my ass, naked, began to freeze to the ice melt. Almost involuntarily, before he could get it in, I jumped back up. Angry, he stormed off – and didn't come back. Ever.

The last month of pregnancy passed in mourning. As soon as he stopped calling, my parents caught on, and affirmed – again – that they would not raise, or babysit, *"his child."*

They reminded me – again – that I must finish school (they disallowed the GED I could have passed on the spot), and that I would need a job *and* daycare. This was *"my"* sin. If I did not *"sign"* my baby *"away,"* I would be responsible to cover every waking minute of my child's life, without help – without my own parents – without my baby's father. . . . This was *"why fornication"* was *"forbidden."* I had *"known better,"* and I must *"pay the price."*

Nothing in my life ever hurt as much as that labor. Part of it was the dilation process – the 8 pound, 6 ounce, baby's head, being slammed into my cervix for 17 unbroken hours. But more of it was that I didn't want it to come out. As soon as it was born, they would whisk it away, and I would be alone – again – forever. I fought each contraction, trying to hold back, trying to hold my baby in.

But nature won, and then I was pushing, and it slipped through my birth canal, and they held it aloft, and pronounced it a girl – and I *saw* her – and she looked *at* me. And our eyes locked. . . .

And she looked *like* me – and *like Dan*. . . . She did have his dark eyes and jet black curls.

And they wrapped her apparition into a receiving blanket, and rushed her out the door – to her other mother.

My father made sure her new parents were *"in The Faith."*

I've never forgotten my daughter's face – or her eyes that locked with mine for mere nanoseconds – frozen in time. And I've never had a moment when the thought of her didn't bring me to tears. And I've never stopped wondering, *Is she happy? Were they good to her? Is she alright? Does she forgive me?*

~~~

10. THE FORCE OF SOCIAL MOVEMENTS

As demonstrated, the decriminalization of contraceptive information and the advent of the birth control pill, were major forces for social change in the status of women. Contraception is, indeed, "a prerequisite to the liberation of women."[147]

From the early 1950s through the mid- to late-1970s, many social movements were active and vocal in the United States, including: the African American Civil Rights Movement, the Black Power Movement, the student-led Anti-(Vietnam)War/Peace Movement, and rising Gay Liberation and Lesbian Movements. The combined effect was to swell the ranks of social movements with counter-cultural constituents, and thus render the establishment political machine vulnerable to the demands for change of those multiple social movements.

Another active and influential movement to rise at that time was the

---

[147] Gazit, Chana & David Steward. (dir.). 17Feb2003. PBS. *American Experience: The Pill.* WGBH-TV.

Women's Liberation Movement. [148]

During the Second World War, middle-class and upwardly-mobile White women were encouraged to enter wage labor, for the sake of the war effort. As the war ended, they were then pushed back with a wave of post-war, government, domestic propaganda that sold them marriage and family and domesticity in the suburbs – with a full compliment of electric household appliances. Over time, many of these women grew more and more discontent with their lives. They did not find the relative lack of autonomy, and the anonymity and isolation, of housewifery and childrearing – with no personally acquired income (*even in a family, money is power, in this case, the power of the husband over the wife*) – as idyllic as the 1950s sitcoms made it appear – a fact Betty Friedan captured in her text, *The Feminine Mystique*, when she labeled their cognitive dissonance as *"the problem that has no name."*[149]

That text, and others, were circulated hand to hand, generating grassroots activism. In addition, coverage of media events planned by social movement organizations, like the *National Organization of Women* (NOW), helped to swell the ranks of Movement constituents with housewives questioning their own life courses, and with college-aged women disenchanted by their gendered treatment in the Civil Rights, New Left and Anti-(Vietnam)War/Peace movements.

---

[148] They called themselves the Women's Liberation Movement. Media ascribed them as Feminist. When we look at the Suffrage Movement and the mid-20th Century Wormen's Liberation Movement, we often call them the First and Second waves of feminism. Black feminists of the 2nd Wave also sometimes referred to themselves as Womanist. In each wave, then and since, Black and Latina Feminists have critiqued the privilege and narrow issues of White feminists. In-movement critique is a valuable facet of any movement. However, even though White women got/get the majority of the media press, in actuality, both the 1st and 2nd Waves, and each wave since, were/are led and forwarded by women of all races and ethniciteis. Each wave of Women's Rights activism is, and has in actuality been, multiracial, multiethnic, and intersectional.

[149] Friedan, Betty. 1963. The Feminine Mystique. New York: W.W. Norton & Company.

Along with women's increasing expectations about access to *meaningful* paid work and access to higher education, heterosexual women's control of their own reproduction was dramatically altered by the creation of the birth control pill in 1960, and the 1965 U.S. Supreme Court *Griswold v Connecticut*[150] ruling that legalized both contraception,[131] and access to information about contraception. Having a reliable, female-controlled, form of birth control (condoms and withdrawal are both controlled by men), empowered women to organize and to undertake actions (like pressing class action lawsuits)[152] to force employers to allow them to retain their jobs after marriage. It also changed the sexual game plan. Sex outside of marriage became more possible. Given that the discovery of antibiotics had all-but-conquered syphilis and gonorrhea, and that viral STIs (like herpes, and HPV, and HIV) were still essentially unheard of – with the pill it was possible, for the first time, for women to have casual sex without fear.[153] This sparked the demand for an end to the sexual double standard and, in keeping with other social change, the time became known as the "Sexual Revolution."

In this era, two other forces also coalesced.

---

[150] *Griswold v. Connecticut*, 381 U.S. 479 *(Estelle T. Griswold and C. Lee Buxton v. Connecticut)*. 7Jun1965. https://supreme.justia.com/cases/federal/us/381/479/

[151] Years of work by social movement organizations like *Planned Parenthood*, and by activist Margaret Sanger and others, had resulted in both the legalization of and the dissemination of information about contraception (*Griswold v Connecticut* 1965), and the creation of an oral contraceptive (1960). www.pbs.org/wgbh/amex/pill/peopleevents

[152] As exemplified by: Warren, James. 10 July 1986. Airline Ends Sex-bias Suit For $33 Million. http://articles.chicagotribune.com/1986-07-10/news/8602190033_1_flight-attendants-eeoc-discrimination; Barry, Kathleen. 2006. A History of Flight Attendants: Timeline of Flight Attendants' Fight Against Discrimination. FemininityinFlight.com. http://femininityinflight.com/activism.html

[153] Gazit, Chana & David Steward. (dir.). 17Feb2003. PBS. *American Experience: The Pill.* WGBH-TV.

~ ~ ~

Michael's Girl

A Narrative

I told him I was on the pill. I didn't so much intentionally lie. I just wanted to keep him close, and a rubber seemed like a distance I didn't want between us, and pregnancy didn't really seem possible. I mean, I tried to be careful and calculate what I knew of my times of the month. At first, I wasn't really ready to be pregnant, but I did want to marry him, and we were in 12th grade, and if it happened, it happened. But mostly I just wanted to feel *him* – inside me. *Him*. Not a barrier.

The threat of pregnancy seemed like some "Old Nun's Tale," like all the crap they put out about virgins giving birth, and naked baby cherubim and seraphim fluttering around the throne of God – like the pomp and circumstance of little girls with azalea flower crowns and bouquets of tulips marching behind a giant plaster statue of the blue-robed Queen of Heaven – overblown, exaggerated, unreal.

As did his saying that he was gay. . . .

It seemed so simple then, in my 17-year-old brain. I was in love with him. His dark shiny eyes. His deep black curls. That strong, but not overstated, Italian nose. Even though, at 5'9", he was not truly tall enough for me when I wore heels, I figured he wasn't done growing, and I thought – for a boy like him – I could give up heels if I had to.

And he was funny. Sweet and sensitive, but still strong and muscled. Even if not in stature, I could definitely look up to him – as a person.

And he came from a good family. His father was a hard-working local businessman, and his mother had dedicated her life to raising him and his sisters. She was all I wanted to be – a wife and a mother – the wife of a good man, the mother of stable children.

She was nothing like my mother. And his dad was so unlike mine.

After our third date, when he took me to meet his extended family, I was immediately struck by the kindness and joviality of their clan. While the wine flowed freely, both at dinner and after, no one seemed to drink too much. And they laughed with a tone of understanding when they rehearsed the family story of the time Michael snuck a bottle of his father's homemade wine out to the garage freezer, to chill, but his mother stayed up later than usual, so that by the time he brought it in, it exploded as it defrosted, all over the family room linoleum – the alcohol cutting a hole through his mother's 10-years of painstakingly-laid, weekly floor wax – a tell-tale sign he had no means to cover. Busted.

I never experienced that kind of gentleness at home. At home, I hid from the rages – from the father who never knew when to stop hitting the bottle – or when to stop hitting my mother – or me.

I wanted nothing more than for Michael, and I, to be lost in a world of our own. I fantasized about a desert island, his muscles rippling in the sunlight as he chopped wood to warm our sand cave just off the beach, or to roast the game he'd hunted. And I touched myself nightly to the memory of his kisses and of his hands straying inside the confines of my shirt.

What did he mean – *gay*???

This hunk of a boy I'd pursued like a steak dinner for the starving! Gay!?!

It was preposterous! Some sort of pretense! Had some other girl caught his eye? Was this some new and glaring rejection – just another in a lifetime of abandonments? He had to be lying, saying it only to get away. *What was wrong with me? How had I driven him away – too?*

There had been Jack in the 9th grade and Tom in the 10th.

Had I given it up too soon? I'd never slept with Jack, but Tom had walked away as soon as he'd gotten "*it*." But Michael had stayed – had dated me all year – till I thought we were solid.

Sobbing, he told me of his feelings for men. He broke down in my arms, and I tried to comfort him. It tore me up inside – this holding him while his chest shook with shame, even as his pain twisted the knife in my own gut.

He didn't look gay. . . . I mean, he was pretty, sort of extra pretty, but he was strong – even a little gruff. He knew all about sports. He grew up playing catch in the side yard with his dad, and baseball with the boys in the neighborhood.

He "*couldn't tell*" his dad, he sobbed. His father had already lost one son to crib death. He "*couldn't bear*" to be the reason he lost another son – to shame.

He "*didn't know anyone gay. . . .*"

There was that one family story about the *fanook* uncle who moved to the West coast and was never heard from again. One aunt said she saw his name in some credits at the end of a movie once, when she, at her psychologist's suggestion, had hired a babysitter to go out on a date night with her husband. But he didn't *know* anyone gay, and the church said it sent you to hell, and I have to admit – the last few times we made love, I started to pray that the nuns were right – that it was easy to get pregnant, and that one of his sperm cells would meet one of my eggs and that insemination would take.

And of course, we were still doing it. *I* was doing it to comfort him as he sobbed. And it was easy to get him there, since we'd been there before. He just couldn't be *frocio*! He was able to perform – with me!

By the time I realized that my prayers had been answered, we were no longer boyfriend and girlfriend – and we had quit doing "*it.*"

By then, I was his closest friend, since I was the only friend who knew that he *thought he was gay.*

In truth, I just thought he was losing his mind – having a psychotic break – or fleeing *from me*. And by then, I had traced new lines, deeper lines, into my forearm, with my father's straight razor, thinking about how easy it would be to slip and go deeper. By then, I was running to the john every morning, losing the breakfast I hadn't consumed.

I didn't tell him at first.

I wasn't sure what he'd do.

I hoped it meant he would stay.

He was talking about escaping, just after graduation, to Miami. He had some relatives there, and he'd heard there were gay bars – *maybe even* a gay community. . . .

I couldn't believe he'd even think about leaving that lovely home as "escaping," or that he would consider doing "that" to his wonderful parents, but by Easter he was weaving daily tales of an early summer road trip to visit family – a trip from which he'd never return.

One night, as we met again to talk about his "dreams," while his parents and mine still thought we were on a "date," he noticed. My belly was starting to show.

His flash of anger was molten and livid. "*You told me you were on the pill!*" he shouted, jumping out of the car and stomping off in the direction of the water tower under which we had parked. When I followed him, I saw his face shatter. He "*wasn't ready for this!*" Wouldn't "*ever be ready*" for this. "*Wasn't straight.*" "*Couldn't,*" wouldn't, "*marry me!*"

I'd never seen him yell before, but even then, his upbringing showed. He kept his hands to himself and didn't call me names. Which was more than I could say for my father, who had put me out on the street, bruising both face and belly, just earlier that evening.

Michael took me home to his mom.

I didn't tell her he said he was "*gay*." And he didn't tell.

She iced my bruises. Consoled him, the way a mother might console a straight son, with promises of help that would allow him to still pursue his career. She promised the years of help that would allow him to become "*a man*," and get a "*good job*," and provide for the family he'd begun – *with me*.

Hope sang in my chest as she made space for me in his sister's room, who was "*off to college*," and before we turned in, she called my mom to tell her I was alright and suggested they meet for coffee, tomorrow.

I finished my senior year in their house. Michael's mom and my mom discussed plans for a quiet ceremony. Just the priest and the most intimate circles of relatives. Dinner for 10 just after. They booked the church and the local diner for late-June.

On June 12th, Michael's parents and my mom watched as we – each in our turn – marched across the platform to accept our diplomas. My father didn't attend. To this day, I'm not sure if he stayed home to protest my pregnancy, well hidden under my graduation robe, or if my mother, quietly, uninvited him. I didn't care.

On the morning of June 14th, Michael was gone. We found out later, when he called from the road, he'd taken a long-distance bus. He stayed with the relatives in Miami, almost until my due date, then disappeared into "*The Life*" – with a lover he'd met at the bar.

Both my mom and Michael's mom were there when I pushed our son into the world. I lived with his mom the baby's whole first year. It was safer than being around my dad. And when I found a job, she offered to babysit every minute I needed. For a good three years, she did 40 or more hours a week, until I got on my feet, and Michael, Jr. got into preschool.

Michael, Sr. never came back to meet him.

We got occasional reports. A hospital called his parents once, when a lover had broken four of his ribs and left him unconscious. And he let them know when a play he'd written got produced at a small Miami theater.

I did marry. Twice. And thanks in part to his mom's ready guidance, I avoided marrying a man like *my* dad.

Both of my husbands were kind – like Michael's family. Both were good to his son, and the four more children I had between them.

The last time I saw Michael, and the first time his son saw him, he was in his casket.

A hospital had called again to say he was ill, and his mother had flown down to visit – then flown back with his body.

She managed to get there just before he lost consciousness to AIDS-related pneumocystis pneumonia. He died far enough into the epidemic that hospitals and funeral homes had begun to get past their fears, and to, again, treat the sick and the dying with dignity. So, we were able to have a viewing, and the priest pronounced his magic words, and Michael's parents – and his son – buried him in the hallowed ground of the Catholic cemetery – no questions asked.

A portion of my heart went into that ground with him – the portion he'd exiled to Florida all those years before.

By then, his son was old enough to be one of his pallbearers – joined by the friends and ex-lovers who had flown in from Florida for the funeral.

~ ~ ~

Women's Narratives & Doctors of Conscience

Women began to write, and publish their own narratives, in periodicals, about the dangers of illegal abortion.[154] These narratives were careful to affirm the beliefs of most Americans about the "proper place" of women and their role as mothers.[155] The Pro-Choice narratives of the 1960s created the atmosphere in which women's need, American women's need, for reproductive choice (for reliable, female-controlled contraception and for safe, sanitary, skilled, legal abortion[156]) became socio-politically compelling.[157] In that illegal context, female authors told the truth about the horrors and risks of back-alley abortions. In their narratives, the women seeking abortion were women who, under other circumstances, would desire to be (or already were, many times over) mothers. Couched in terms readers could empathize with, these narratives told tales of "Good Women" (women who valued motherhood), who, in bad circumstances, were driven to desperation over their real need to deny or delay motherhood at that time, or, under specific given circumstances, like rape, or unwed status. Hence, the illegal abortion narrative centered on the victim of rape, the teen who had made a mistake and shouldn't have her entire life derailed, or the mother of many whose overwhelming circumstances compelled her to the brink of despair about another pregnancy, or another pregnancy at that time. Working within this frame of "The Good Woman," these narratives

---

[154] Condit 1990
[155] ibid
[156] ibid
[157] ibid

were able to depict the tragedy of the abortion gone wrong because of the greed, callousness, or incompetence of the abortionist.

These narratives coalesced with a growing dissatisfaction among doctors, at governmental limitations on their freedom to prescribe the procedures that they, and their patients, deemed best.[158] Doctors were becoming more and more dissatisfied with the restrictions on their diagnostic roles in relation to abortion.[159] The advent of antibiotics, and the improvement in their surgical techniques, had also increased their ability to provide safe abortions. Thus, doctors tired of watching their patients die of illegal abortions, when they could have provided safe ones. At the same time, many came to resent their mandated[160] role in facilitating the deathbed confessions of the victims of back-alley abortions (mandated as part of reporting illegal abortion providers). Despite threats of loss of license or prosecution for breaking a medically-restrictive law, many doctors balked against the restrictions on their ability to provide adequate and appropriate health care to their female patients and found ways to circumvent the law.

In addition, many doctors and medical students faced the specter of the women who were dying – by the thousands – in their hospitals, of hemorrhage and septicemia, and other effects, of poorly done, "back-alley," procedures. Therefore, a goodly portion of those "doctors of conscience"[161] began to come to consciousness about this issue, and state-by-state, doctors joined those pushing for legislative reform. Before the Supreme Court heard the *Roe v. Wade* case, the combination of women voicing their experiences, and of doctors and lawyers calling for legislative reform,[162]

---

[158] Joffe 1995
[159] ibid
[160] ibid
[161] ibid
[162] ibid

resulted in referendums bringing legislative reform in a number of states. The realities of hospital deaths, of patient and doctor interrogations by police, of published reform narratives, of the economic shifts of women's workplace participation, and of the social changes (created by the increasing public discussion of sex and contraception – because of academic work like that done by Kinsey, and by Masters and Johnson – created an overriding paradigm shift in both public and professional attitudes – so that by the time the Supreme Court heard *Roe v. Wade*, a shift in the Court's understanding had been necessitated. Thus, the stage was set by 1973 for *Roe* to remove, with limits, the 70+ years of legal restrictions against abortion.

~~~

Polar Shifts

A Narrative

The girl I fell in love with was a full-blown woman.

She was educated. A physician.

Mira was motivated. She was at the top of her profession, a surgeon with skills noted by her colleagues, staff, hospital administration, and patients. She was the up-and-coming surgeon profiled in the medical magazines as one of the "Top 40 Under 40," winning awards, having her hand shaken in congratulations and thanked for her prodigious skills – for the lives she'd helped, for the lives she'd already saved.

She had acquired the trappings. Two sprawling houses, one in town and one on the lakeshore. Two cars, both expensive, one for the warmer, sportier days, the other for the Chicago blizzards that might otherwise keep her from her appointed rounds.

She was beautiful. Built. Trim. Muscled. A regular at the gym – bench pressing 145 pounds. Tall. 5'8" in her stocking feel, 5'10" to 6'foot tall in heels.

She was done childbearing. She came with a ready-made family – one son, nearly-grown. All the offspring she wanted. Which was also, all the children I wanted.

Even the story of how she'd continued her education and built her career, despite being a single mother, was enough to make people feel they should stand up and salute. She had truly come up from under, no matter the obstacles in her way. She had fought and scrabbled her way through undergrad and into medical school, then up through the ranks of the students and into a prestigious surgical internship and residency, then into her first and second positions – so that by the time I came along, she had it all.

All – except a man.

And so, I gladly added my accomplishments to her own. I had my own education, my own career, and my own weight bench pressed at the gym. The mirror told me I looked alright, and though – new to the area, I hadn't yet bought a house by the time I met her – I was working with a realtor and stepping up my game.

So, Mira and I became an item. Over the first few months, we spent more and more time together. I mean, such as we had. We were both quite busy, but when we could, we were there – together. We hiked, and we dined, and we took in culture – sometimes with her son, sometimes without.

Gradually, our lives blended, until it seemed nonsensical for me to buy a separate house, and at her insistence, I simply moved in.

Furtively, I tried to gather a feel for her taste in jewelry and took the plunge. I bought a ring, took her out for Valentine's, and by the warmth of candle glow, dropped to one knee – nearby restaurant patrons cheering me on.

Our engagement was magical. I had done well. I had chosen a ring she loved.

And she loved me.

And we set a date two years in the future, to give her, and her mother, time to plan the wedding a "Top 40 Over 40" deserved – press and all. It would be the event of the season, two years hence, and her *by-then* grown, son would give her away.

Through the years, she'd had trouble with hormonal contraceptives. She didn't like the effects on her. And once engaged, our condom use felt out of place. Increasingly, the barrier felt more and more intrusive. But, without the hormones – and with the time her body had rejected a copper I.U.D. – we didn't have much else, and so, we were left with withdrawal.

Which also had its issues. I thought I was reasonably good at it, but it is difficult – stopping and shifting the action, just when it starts to feel best. . . . judging just how far you can push it. . . . *Coitus Interruptus.*

Once or twice, I didn't quite *"time it"* right.

And whenever I failed – at anything – I saw a glimmer of anger around the edges of her placid veneer.

But she would just shudder, and get out of bed and douche, even as she fussed to herself about how douching is not an effective contraceptive. And then, she would calculate with the calendar, whether or not it were worth the hormonal hit to her body to send me to the store for emergency contraception to try to stop her ovulation.

But my sometimes miss-at-withdrawal was not our only problem.

Increasingly, I became aware that there were times she simply was not in charge of her emotions. I wasn't always sure if she could have been and was just behaving badly, or if there was a psychological disorder underlying the anger she began, more frequently, to display. But sometimes, I became fearful that she would cross some unforeseen, undefined line, and our relationship would wreck on the shores of some unseen outcropping of underwater boulders.

Her son and I developed a relationship. Since I wasn't his dad, I didn't go there, but I did try to offer an adult male role model and my honest, mentoring, friendship. Sometimes, I helped with homework. Other times, I took him to the gym. Other times, I took him out to buy a present for his mom – spotting him a $20 for Mother's Day, and a hundred for her birthday and for Christmas. So I began to flinch, when I felt she was too hard on him.

Apparently, in her childhood home, screaming was the approved means of motivating a child to fulfill their responsibilities. But her yelling triggered all my years of being under one parental thumb or another. I had not forgotten what it felt like to be that child. . . .

It also made me worry about what would happen when she got mad at me. *Would she do me that way?*

At first, she never yelled. And then, she only yelled at her son and only when it seemed somewhat justified – like when his music was too loud, or his homework was undone, or the trash was piling up in the kitchen.

But about six months into living together, I noticed that the yelling often seemed less justified and more incessant, and that some of it had begun to be directed at me.

I had a conversation with her. I explained my complicated

childhood relationship with being yelled at, and my determination in adulthood never to suffer such treatment again.

She continued.

I made an appointment with a couples' therapist, forced the time slot into our busy calendars, and nearly dragged her in to *"tell a stranger"* about *"our private business."* She spent the session cross-legged, crossed-armed, and sullen – while I tried to fill the space by telling the therapist my history of, and objection to, yelling and verbal insults.

She barely nodded a "yes" to returning the next week, and by session three, she simply refused to get in the car.

I paid the therapist for services not rendered and cancelled our future appointments, and at home, found myself – inadvertently – yelling back.

I guess I thought we could still work it out. Or I had not yet lost all sense of hope. Or love makes us all a little crazy. But I did not just break up and move out. Instead, we fought, then had wild make-up sex, then had a good week or two in which she was very apologetic and kind – like she was at the first – and then, the tension started rising again, and she exploded once more.

I spent a lot of time trying to ascertain how much of it was me. Sometimes I journaled, to allow myself reflection on, and distance from, the situation – to *"learn what I thought by seeing what I said."*[163]

In the journaling, it was her fault, not mine.

In the arguments, she reframed my concerns into my errors, and it was all my fault – none of it hers.

But we – or at least, I – continued to make up, to make love, to try to connect, to attempt to reconnect, and to search for what

---

[163] "*I write because I don't know what I think until I read what I say.*" (Flannery O'Connor)

was lost – or what I thought had been lost – even as I began to face what had never actually been.

The truth was, I was lost

And then, one of the times when I failed to pull out – and when, by her calculation, douching should have been sufficient – took.

Given the fragility of our relationship, and of her mental stability, I wanted the chance to, at least, talk through our options.

She had always said she could never "kill a baby." Along with avoiding the pill, she opposed abortion.

Trying to open the opportunity to discuss it, I made another appointment with the couples' therapist – then mailed another check for services not rendered.

She wouldn't talk. Instead, she just sat and sobbed – or yelled.

She insisted that it was her decision, her decision alone, and that there was no decision. It was already a done-deal. My sperm had met her egg, and her version of deity had already created a human soul, and – as she did when she had her son *"too young"* – she would carry to term and pay the price of *"God's will"* and raise *"her child"* to adulthood – even though, now, she was *"too old."*

Since we were still engaged, it didn't compute when she spoke about her future as a single, not a married, parent.

And, despite her age, she refused amniocentesis and any idea of checking the embryo for defects. In her theology, whatever "God" had created, had a right to life – no matter who would suffer or how much.

Conception was *"God-ordained."*

Yet, we had agreed from the start that she was done, and she knew from the first date that I didn't want children. And we weren't exactly keeping her religion's rules about premarital sex. . . .

As she made her pronouncements about keeping it, I began to adjust to the idea. I worried about her mental state. Worried that her increasingly obvious mental health issues would be a detriment to any child we brought into the world together, so I grew used to the idea of becoming a very present, very protective dad. I hoped it would get its emotional-stability genes from me – not from my family tree particularly – but also, not from the mother gestating it in her womb.

I bought an infant carrier. We ordered a crib online – a really nice one that could convert into a toddler bed. I painted the room she decided would be the nursery. She chose a pale yellow.

I wondered who in my family I should inform.

I drove her to the obstetrician, who assigned a due date, and we began to count the weeks.

We moved the wedding date up, and she talked about something more low key – quieter, more private, more intimate.

At week 11, I came home from a business trip to find Mira, stony-faced and silent in our bed. In the bathroom trash, face up, lay a feminine napkin, hospital-sized – used. I rushed back into the bedroom, heartbroken at the thought of a miscarriage, ready to console her for our mutual loss.

Quietly, firmly, she said, "*I murdered it. I decided I just can't do it. God will punish me, but not before I punish myself.*"

The floor tumbled out from under me. My heart leapt into my throat, even as my stomach chased the receding floor, into a bottomless pit.

I think I mouthed the word, "*What?*"
Maybe I said, "*What the . . . ?*"

She rolled over and spent the night, silent, refusing to answer. For all the response my questions or presence evoked, I might as well have been the wind, or the sound of a train in the quiet distance.

In the morning, she got up and went to work. She kept a shorter schedule that week, then moved forward like nothing had happened.

At dinner, three nights after my business trip, Mira turned to her son and said, "*I miscarried your baby brother or sister. We won't discuss it again,*" and then went back to chewing.

His face froze.

I finally saw her narcissism.

She had the right to an abortion all along. It was her body. She was still in the first trimester. I would have been there to help raise it, but I hadn't wanted to be a father. She was the one that would have to be pregnant for nine months, give birth, lactate, and go through post-partum recovery. Abortion had been my first response. We *were* too old, our relationship too tenuous, and neither one of us had wanted a child. I would have helped her make the appointment, driven her, comforted her, and loved her, through it.

She also had every right to choose to carry to term. Whether I wanted her to, or not. I didn't wear a condom. I had lost my sperm inside her. So once she had conceived, she had the right to choose to carry. I had no right to force or demand an abortion. So, I had adjusted. I had gotten into it. I had come to want that child – our child – my child. I had decided to step up to the plate and be the dad I never had. I had even signed up, on the quiet, for parenting classes. I became determined to do it right, to be the best bumper between our mutual parental ignorance and our child's chances at a balanced, safe, and happy life.

And she had taken me along for that ride. Emotionally, she had ridden over me, ridden through me, and refused to so much as discuss either option with me – pressing me to follow wherever she – and her rights to her body – led. Even if it led to a child with birth defects, because – at a relatively advanced reproductive age – she refused genetic testing.

But, after she had gotten me primed to accept – and to love – a child, whatever child we had – she had unilaterally ripped it away from me.

I didn't have a right to force her to be on the pill. And once I spilled my sperm, I didn't have a right of final determination to what she did with her body – to whether or not she carried.

And rightly so.

No one should be able to force another human being to go through an unwanted pregnancy, childbirth, and 18 years of parenting an underage dependent.

I had had a right to a condom, but I gave that up, when despite my bad sense of timing, I had trusted hers.

But I also had a right to a partner who considered my desires, and my feelings. I had a right to be taken into account by the woman I loved.

I took a week off work, rented a storage bin and a room, and packed quietly. To avoid her screaming, I did most of it when she had to be at work. And I hired movers to show up on Friday and liberate me, and my possessions, from her home while she was scheduled to be in surgery.

I left, thanking the Universe, that it all happened before we had tied the legal knot.

The biggest loss I still feel is my relationship with her son.

That – and the hit to my sense of trust – in relationships.

~~~

Backlash Against the (Reproductive)

Liberation of Women*

A backlash against women's rights is nothing new in American history. Indeed, it's a recurring phenomenon: it returns every time women[164] begin to make some headway toward equality.... An accurate charting of American women's progress through history might look more like a corkscrew tilted slightly to one side, its loops inching closer to the line of freedom with the passage of time— but, like a mathematical curve approaching infinity, never touching its goal. The American woman is trapped on this asymptotic spiral, turning endlessly through the generations, drawing ever nearer to her destination without ever arriving. Each revolution promises to be "*the revolution*" that will free her from the orbit, that will grant her, finally, a full measure of human justice and dignity. But each time, the spiral turns her back just short of the finish line."[165]

In 1991, Susan Faludi argued that, with even small advances in women's rights, backlash is swift and reactionary. She writes,

"when feminism itself becomes the tide, the opposition doesn't simply go along with the reversal: it digs in its heels, brandishes its fists, builds walls and dams. And its resistance creates countercurrents and treacherous undertows."[166]

She further notes,

---

[164] or any social movement
[165] Faludi 1991:46-47
[166] Faludi 1991: xxi

"A backlash against women's rights is nothing new in American history. Indeed, it's a recurring phenomenon: it returns every time women begin to make some headway toward equality, a seemingly inevitable early frost to the culture's brief flowerings of feminism."[167]

As Faludi argues, the legalization of abortion brought a swift response. As the tide of change built, the initial response was pre-empted by the Roman Catholic Church, which issued doctrinal statements against *all* non-procreative sex and against *all* forms of contraception (which they labeled "*artificial*").[168]

But by the late 1970s and early 1980s, backlash came as well from a rising tide of Protestant Fundamentalists and Evangelicals.

Not founded till the early part of the 20th Century, Christian Fundamentalism had been a movement on the margins of Mainline Christianity until the 1950s. But fundamentalists[169] and evangelicals made studied use of radio, and later of television, and it proved a very effective method of selling (mass marketing) their understanding of the "gospel"[170] – and their worldview.

Holding to a doctrine of scriptural inerrancy, Fundamentalists/ Evangelicals and Pentecostals/Charismatics (who, many times, call themselves "non-denominational") find that their scriptures teach a gender

---

[167] Faludi 1991: 46

[168] Pope Paul VI. *Humanae Vitae*. 25Jul1968. http://www.webcitation.org/5xI2Wz6n5.

[169] Not a pejorative term. Christian fundamentalists use the term in reference to themselves. Their movement began as an early 20th Century response to Darwinian evolution. They hold to five "fundamentals:" the virgin birth of Christ, Christ's substitutionary death, Christ's physical resurrection, the second coming of Christ and the *inerrancy* (divine inspiration and divine preservation as error free) of the Bible. Fundamentalism includes many denominations and independent congregations. There are distinctions between fundamentalists and evangelicals, but theologically, they are also large areas of overlap.

[170] Also know as "the good news," the gospel is the message that Christ came to die as a substitutionary sacrifice for human sin, thereby assuaging divine wrath and redeeming humankind.

ideology of male dominance and female submission[171] – both in the church congregation and (most especially) in the home & family.

The rising tide of Women's Liberation, and the freedoms brought to women by reliable contraception (i.e. the ability to have sex without the fear of pregnancy or the need of the "protection" of marriage), were perceived as a threat to *The Moral Order*.

Abortion was the icing on an already toppling cake.

Television preachers used airtime to address the social issues of the day.

Specific men, including but certainly not limited to Jerry Falwell and Pat Robertson, stepped to the fore, hypothesizing that as American citizens, "*Christians*,"[172] and their interests, had a right to be represented in government. Organizations like the *Moral Majority*[173] and the *Christian Coalition*[174] became a political force that has come to be called the *Religious Right*. They countered the survivor's narratives of the horrors of the illegal abortion (with its focus on the realities of what ill-timed and unwanted reproduction, and botched back-alley abortions, cost adolescent and adult women), with an ahistorical narrative[175] that constructs America as a "Christian" – rather than a Religiously-Pluralist nation with freedom of

---

[171] They often couch it in terms of "complementarianism," which is the idea that the unequal "traditional" gender roles – as part of God's design – allow *dominant* men and *subordinate* women to "complement" each other.

[172] When speaking of "Christians" it is not uncommon for various groups, including fundamentalists, evangelicals, and Pentecostals, to speak as if their own group encompasses all "Christians."

[173] Founded by the Southern Baptist television minister and pastor, the Rev. Jerry Falwell of Lynchburg, Virginia, in 1979

[174] Founded by Pat Robertson, along with his Christian Broadcasting Network (CBN), as a means of informing fundamentalist/evangelical Christians of the voting records of candidates for public office – specifically on issues like abortion and gay rights.

[175] Condit 1990

religion for more than Christians – and created a narrative of the "murder" of an **autonomous, baby-like**, zygote – **fully human, ensouled, and sentient from the moment of conception.**

But the *Religious Right* did not/does not just lightly tap "religious fanaticism or mere opportunism"[176] for the purpose of preaching Christ or spreading the Fundamentalist/ Evangelical/ Pentecostal gospel. Intent on gaining power and reclaiming America for God, through "mobilizing a nationwide mass following," the *Religious Right* located "sexual, reproductive, and [heterosexual] family issues," most specifically their opposition to abortion, at the "substantive core" of its politics.[177]

For Right-Wing politicians, this same fight against modernity has functioned as a "primary vehicle" through which they have "achieved their ascent to state power."[178] The Anti-Choice ("Right-To-Life") Movement is "a battering ram in a much broader offensive against feminism, non-traditional (LGBTQ) families, teenage sexuality, "single-headed" (teenage and divorced mother non-traditional families), the welfare state, socialism, and every other target of the *Right.*"[179]

While the *Religious Right* has pursued the formation of "a moral cartel to use state power to define the social role of women," and to "validate" "their moral outlook" (their Fundamentalist/ Evangelical/ Pentecostal worldview), via "legitimating political institutions,"[180] the *Political Right* is intent on using the political sphere as a means to reinforce traditionalism and to resist the changes in women's roles.[181] Reacting to changes in "real

---

[176] Petchesky 1981: 206-07
[177] ibid
[178] Petchesky 1981: 207
[179] Petchesky 1984: 242
[180] Barry & Popkin in Luker 1984
[181] Faludi 1991

material conditions"[182] – for which it blames feminism[183] and gay rights – for the Right, the actual changes brought by the success of these movements (Women's and Gay Liberation) have touched "deep lying fears"[184] – so that fighting changes in the status of women (through fighting abortion) and opposing gay rights – has catapulted both their leaders (and their voting block powers) to "national political" prominence.[185]

For the Anti-Choice *Religious Right*, two scapegoats – **abortion** and contraception (as a stand in for Women's Liberation), and **gay rights** (LGBTQ*-affirming (lesbian, gay, bisexual, transgender, queer) anti-discrimination and relationship-recognition laws (as a stand in for patriarchal marriage [male dominance/female submission]), became the paramount boogiemen. These two issues were seen to "pose the ultimate challenges to the cultural bond between sexuality and procreation"[186] – and therefore, to patriarchal control (via fathers/ male partners/ husbands) of the sexuality of "their" wives and daughters.

With contraception and access to early term abortion, women were empowered to not *need* the "protection" or "provision" of a male personage in order to meet their (and their children's) need for subsistence. With the help of contraception, they could control the number of their pregnancies (and of the children they brought-to-term) well-enough that they could also work, and thus, "eat the bread of independence."[187]

---

[182] Petchesky 1981: 237
[183] Petchesky 1981: 236
[184] Petchesky 1981: 237
[185] ibid
[186] Stacey 1991:12
[187] Susan B. Anthony

At core, the abortion controversy is a **"conflict of worldviews,"** between conservatives and progressives, **that centers around women's roles.**[188] "The abortion crisis," and LGBTQ* "rights, primarily speak to the relations between men and women."[189] With the ability to have *out* and *open* same-sex relationships, a more egalitarian model of relationship might come to the fore – no longer based on the hierarchical *domination* and *submission* of unequal heterosexual gender roles – but one in which (since same-sex couples are actually both of the same-sex) neither partner is the God-ordained "head," and neither is the God-ordained follower.[190]

The traditional family, for which religious conservatives began to fight in earnest, was one in which a man "took" a virgin bride, ruled (perhaps kindly, but definitively) "over" her, impregnated her frequently, earned their daily bread while she did *all* of the housework and childcare (whether or not she also worked outside of the home), was promised obedience by his wife in the marriage ceremony, was given obedience by (or took obedience from) his wife and children on a daily basis, had final decision making authority in "his" family, was met at the door each night upon his return with pipe and slippers, was served his dinner, and retired after his meal to relax at the end of his hard day.

Using their television platforms[191] as a trumpet for their theological positions – that "babies" were being "murdered," and that the traditional

---

[188] Luker 1984

[189] Joffe 1985: 27

[190] Fundamentalist/Evangelical/Pentecostals speak often about "the husband being the head of the wife" (Ephesians 5:23 & 1 Corinthians 11:3) and therefore, having "final decision making authority" in the home – especially in cases where the spouses agree (the man is considered to be the one not deceived by the serpent in the garden of Eden (1 Timothy 2:14), and therefore, ordained by God to lead (be "the head of") the woman in any conflict.

[191] Their own radio and television broadcasts, self-publishing, and their Christian television networks, like CBN (Christian Broadcasting Network), PTL (Praise the Lord Network), TBN (Trinity Broadcasting Network), and EWTN (Eternal Word Television Network, Roman Catholic), etc.

family (and, therefore, God's favor on the nation) were being threatened by he Women's and Gay Liberation Movements – the preacher/leaders of the *Religious Right* used their public media presence – and their dogmatic gender theology – to organize their congregants and viewers into a vocal minority – and into a solid voting block determined to "*vote their conscience*" in regard to opposing (and dismantling) abortion rights and lesbian and gay people's forward political motion.

Thus, the litmus test for membership in the "Non-Denominational"/ Fundamentalist/ Evangelical/ Pentecostal Christian churches became:

1. opposition to abortion access and

2. opposition to "gay rights"

    a. opposition to the ability for LGBTQ people to serve openly in the military

    b. opposition to the ordination of LGBTQ ministers and to the inclusion of LGBTQ laity in the full life of the church

    c. opposition to relationship recognition (civil marriage rights) for same-sex/gender couples

By 1980, the *Republican Party*, through its candidate Ronald Reagan, declared its platform to include:

1. opposition to gay rights[192] and

2. opposition to abortion (with a sometimes exception in cases of rape, incest, or medical threat to the life of the mother).

The backlash was entrenched.

---

[192] Which today would include all those who are LGBTQ [lesbian, gay, bisexual, transgender, and queer-identified, and all the socio-political issues they face.

This anti-abortion, anti-gay, pro-(straight)family "current" "is indeed a backlash movement. It is a movement to turn back the tide of the major social movements of the 1960s and 1970s,"[193] and it is "aimed primarily at those organizations and ideas that have most directly confronted patriarchal traditions *regarding the place of women* in society and the dominant norms of heterosexual love and marriage."[194] But:

> The strength and determination of this backlash –
> particularly in regard to abortion [and] homosexuality . . . is
> in part a measure of the effectiveness of the women's and
> gay movements, the extent to which their ideas (and
> various commercial distortions of their ideas) have
> penetrated popular culture and consciousness, if not public
> policy . . . . There is no corner of the society where the
> basic liberal feminist idea of women's "equality" with men
> has not touched people in their daily relationships.[195]

The contraceptive, and social, changes of the 1960s shifted American women's attitudes, economic realities, access to education, personal expectations, views of coupling and parenthood, and control of their own bodies.

The backlash of (religious and political) Traditionalists has been intended as a "highly conscious conservative response" to "broad and changing social conditions" in the status of women.[196]

They seek to "make morally and **legally mandatory"** a "kind of family model" that "has become practically extinct in America,"[197] through a "return to **the values of privatism,**" that **would reduce governmental**

---

[193] Petchesky 1981:234
[194] Petchesky 1981234-35, emphasis mine
[195] Petchesky 1981:235
[196] Petchesky 1981: 234
[197] Petchesky 1981: 235

responsibility for "the welfare and education" of citizens" by throwing it "back onto the resources of the family and the church" (faith-based organizations).[198]

And they seek to "confine sexuality within the strict bounds of heterosexual marriage, and women within a patriarchal version of self-denying motherhood."[199]

In as much as it succeeds (or has succeeded), this reactionary agenda undoes the agenda for human rights. The persistence of this backlash (since the late 1970s) renders the early 21st Century America very different in feel than was the U.S., just after mid-20th Century.

The rise of political conservatism "has at its core a virulent opposition to feminism, which includes "not only . . . concern for the embryo," but also "punitive and repressive responses to sexual "freedom" (straight, gay, bi-, pan-, etc,), and powerful resentments against those who lead lives different from theirs."[200]

---

[198] Petchesky 1981: 234; See also: A&E. (2018). On This Day 7Feb. 2002 President George W. Bush announces plan for "faith-based initiatives." http://www.history.com/this-day-in-history/president-george-w-bush-announces-plan-for-faith-based-initiatives
[199] Petchesky 1981: 234
[200] Joffe 1985: 27

~ ~ ~

Trapped

A Narrative

"You do NOT want to know about "how" your mother and I met! Eat your breakfast."

"But Dad," Serita whined, *"How did you meet and FALL IN LOVE?"*

I didn't know how to tell her. *How do you tell a kid they were a mistake? A ball and chain?*

Just then, her mother came in, caught the tail end of the question, and changed the topic, *"Stop pestering your father, Serita. Go finish your homework."*

"I'm going out for a beer," I told Karen gruffly, and left before Serita came back at her, and their conflict turned into a standoff, and their standoff into a fight that meant the homework never got done.

"How did I meet her mother, indeed!?" I held forth to Bob, my bartender/counselor, as I pumped back my fourth beer. *"It's not how I met her! It's how I married her that still pisses me off! All that romance and shit they feed these girls. Serita better not force some boy into marrying her, or that'll be the first time I raise my hand to her myself, I swear to Christ!"* punctuating my emphasis, slamming my mug on the lacquered bar.

"I hear you, Ed," Bob sighed. *"I had to get married too. Most of us did, back in them days."*

"Well your days were a little before mine, Bob. By my days, the girls were supposed to be doing something about it. Karen was supposed to be on the pill. She wasn't supposed to be having her father, get after my father, to force me into "doing the right

thing!" *Christ, abortion was even legal already. But it wasn't thought of. Not by our parents! I never even got to start god-damn college, so here I am, 30-years-later, and still breaking my back laying bricks in the hot sun. How many more years do they think I can do this? Can I do it through Serita's college? I'm already straining just trying to get Eddie, Jr. through. Maybe she WILL have to get herself knocked up, to catch a man, and forget college. Give me a another cold one!"*

"This one's it, Ed. I'm gonna flag you after this. With the mood you're in, I don't wanna be responsible for Karen's busted lip or Serita's therapy! Karen sure was a pretty thing back then! I'd a done her in a heartbeat. Every guy in the class would a, but you was the one that got her!"

"If I had known then, what I know now – about what it's took to keep her and those two spoiled brats – I'd a kept jerking off and left ya have her. My right hand could a stood me in good stead all these years. In fact, it mostly has. Can't say Karen gives it up much, since she stopped wantin' babies. Been damned near celibate 15 years! I get it once or twice a year, tops. That's all I gets. And maybe some head I pay for, when she's not looking. Thank God, the older we got, the better the porn got. Hey, if I'd a been lucky enough to have her get her hooks into some other guy, 'stead a me, I'd a been about a half-million dollars in the black, instead of 160k in the red."

"Ain't that the truth for all of us!" Jim grunted from around the L of the bar. "If they didn't catch us, they wouldn't a had no one to support their brats, and us guys, all, would a been better off. When they coming out with that pill for men??? I heard the scientists were working on it. Too late for me, but hope they hurry up for my son's sake. If he can keep his sperm, and his money, in his pocket, maybe he can put me up in my old age – and it won't matter all he took along the way."

"Shit, I'll never forget the look on her face, sitting across from me and my parents, in my parents' living room, while her father raged at me for "despoiling" his daughter's virtue. All my father said was, "Eddie-boy, you gone and done it! Guess that makes you a man, just like me, when you was coming along. You're gonna' do the right thing. Go put on your good pants. We're gonna' go down to the rectory and rouse the priest. You already had your damned wedding night. It's time to have the ceremony." And that was that. Karen and I were hitched before bedtime, and she dropped out a school and came to live in my room. She was still giving it up then, but shit, it was hard to have quiet sex right above my parents' ceiling!"

Bob slid Jim another beer, and reached out for his tip, as he shook his head sideways, "Naw, my woman told her ma sooner. So we still had a proper ceremony. We just had an eight pound, nine ounce "preemie!"

Jim nodded vigorously, "Happened so much, no one hardly noticed. If memory serves, a third of the girls in our school never graduated. And only the boys not already hitched ever went off to college."

"Good thing a man could make a real living by the sweat of his brow in those days, or we and those brats would a been some poor m-f-er's! But you know, I really did think Karen was on the pill. I swear, somewhere in the back of that old Woodie, she told me she was. I swear, she wanted it just as bad as I did, and she told me it was alright to cum inside."

Jim laughed, "You were a pretty good catch, Ed! You're father had the business, and your future was set to walk into the day after we marched across the platform. You were never gonna' want for nothin.' And since she didn't have too many kids, Karen got a pretty sweet deal! She's ain't never had to work, and she'll retire on your dime."

"Come on, Bob, give me one more. You can see I've calmed down. I'll go straight to the bed in the guest room, and to my trusty right hand. Karen's safe tonight."

~~~

Misleading By Visuals

(*The Manipulation of the Perception of Fetal Development*)

Along with marketing their ideology via television and radio, another strategy of this backlash movement has been to use images of the fetus to produce a visceral reaction.[201] The Anti-Choice Movement uses images of the embryo that are more developed and baby-like than it would be during the first trimester, when 91% of abortion procedures[202] in the U.S. are performed[203] – skewing the visual imagination by **making embryos appear as small infants, rather than showing the stages of first trimester development in their true light**. This slight-of-hand is meant to amplify the Anti-Choice Movement's alignment with those whose religious beliefs stress that life,[204] in the theological sense, begins at conception – rendering the (actually later-term) fetus a "public presence."[205]

In the giant posters of abortion activists, the images of an essentially full-term human baby – apparently viable and autonomous from the mother – are displayed, hacked apart, lying in pools of blood and bodily fluids – while demonstrators resort to comparisons with the Nazi Holocaust and co-opt the rhetoric of genocide. Scholars, like Rosalind Petchesky, accuse the Anti-Choice Movement of manipulating the size of its images, and the fuzzy images of (non-3D) ultrasounds, in order to manipulate the perception of embryonic development.[206]

---

[201] Petchesky 1987
[202] FoxNews. Fast Facts: U.S. Abortion Statistics. 2003.
http://www.foxnews.com/story/2003/06/17/fast-facts-us-abortion-statistics.html
[203] Petchesky 1987
[204] Life as the possession of a fully human soul, created by Deity, and inviolable
[205] Petchesky 1987 (p.264)
[206] Petchesky 1987

~~~

Misgendered

A Narrative

I felt the first blow – from behind. I had heard their taunting when I got out of my car, but it was broad daylight, and I thought, *Just fuck 'em*, and kept walking. Even though I was tired that day, and I just really wanted to go home to rest, I had stopped for my partner, Justice, to buy them a bottle of their favorite green tea (*Their preferred pronouns are they/them/theirs*). They were thinking the healing properties of green tea might be just what they needed, as they continued recovering from the sore throat they had the weekend before.

The pack of late teen boys at the edge of the parking lot didn't sit well with me, but there were no other spots, so I drove into the open one near them, and started walking toward the strip mall, thirty cars away, with determined purpose. I ignored their calls of "*Dyke*," and "*Bushwhacker*," a little pissed off that they were misgendering me – but not thinking too much of it. It happened pretty much everywhere I went. My partner sometimes asked how I ever felt safe going outside, but it had been true for so long that I'd grown numb.

I would go into restaurants, and sit down for a quiet meal alone, and look up between bites from some game or app on my phone, to find myself actively stared at – by one or more – of the other men in the dining room. As I walked in or out of a public building, any public building, even my job site, strangers would stop and turn – and stay stopped and turned – as I passed them, sometimes rudely calling out, "*Excuse me! Are you*

166

a man? or a woman?"

Apparently, despite my deltoid and bicep development, my chest binding, and my careful study of masculine presentation, I was still too short and round-hipped to fit neatly into their binary category of cisgender male. I was tagged as gender-non-conforming, and people often aren't nice to those who queer their sex/gender categories.

But I wasn't expecting the hit from that board, or the tumble of five guys at once. I can't go deeply into the memory – not because I can't relive it, but because I *can't* relive it. I mean, I'm not unwilling to relive it. I guess.... I just can't, because I can't remember most of it.

I felt that first blow. And I felt the weight of multiple bodies taking me down. Then I lost consciousness.

I have a moment or two of hazy recollection. Something about them shouting, "Pull Its pants down and see if it has a dick." And the sense of buttons popping as my shirtfront tore, but mostly, the next thing I remember Is Justice's tears dropping on my hand, and the bright lights and beeping sounds of my hospital room.

Before I woke up, the hospital did a rape kit, 18 stitches (11 to my scalp and 7 to my right forearm), started me on an antibiotic, and post-exposure HIV prophylaxis, and administered emergency contraception. They found semen from five assailants.

The emergency contraception didn't work. The follow-up GYN[207] said I must have ovulated the day or two before the assault – so the drug couldn't prevent conceiving.

---

[207] gynecologist

Pregnant!

Being assaulted had hurt my manhood – my already fragile sense of self. I always imagined myself able to defend myself.

And the emotional violation of being penetrated in an organ I didn't even relate to – and had never used – had been intense.

But then, having something growing inside me that assailants had planted in hate – in the physical enactment of a hate crime – a "corrective" rape…. Having one of their skeevy cells take root – in an organ that shouldn't even be there – took my sense of the wrongness of my body into a whole new, dysphoric, territory.

Not only was I, as a man born in the wrong body, forced to endure the indignities of monthly cycles and developed breasts – not only had the vagina of this wrong body been subject to invasion – but the uterus that didn't belong *in* me – had the nerve to respond like a female's – and begin to grow the seed of my violators.

The GYN discussed our options, then left Justice and I alone. Justice talked me out of trying to open the medical center's secured 4th floor window.

Clearly, there was no possibility of my carrying a baby to term and escaping the pregnancy sane. Not only would I not have done such a thing voluntarily – it was an impossibility to fathom carrying the assailants' seed to term.

Even if Justice hoped, some day, after we were well-established economically, to adopt and raise a child, the dysphoria simply of being pregnant – compounded by being pregnant by violence – was inexpressibly overwhelming.

When the GYN returned, we asked her for the pills. She

administered the Mifepristone, and I went home with the follow-up Misoprostol.

It was the worst period I ever had, and periods have never been kind to me. Still, it was healing. Once the cramping began, I found myself grateful to, given the circumstances, have gotten the best medical care possible. I, a man, had not been forced, against my will, to become the mother of my rapists' child. Afterward, the importance, for me, of bringing my body more into line with the expectations of the binary world around me – for safety's sake alone – led Justice and I to rework our budget, so I could get access to T[208] and save for top surgery[209] – and, as soon as possible, for a hysterectomy. For my mental health, I had to insure I could never get pregnant again.

~ ~ ~

---

[208] Testosterone
[209] double mastectomy

11. STAGES OF DEVELOPMENT

The truth is that the product of conception takes a long time to turn into a human infant. It goes through many non-human-appearing stages (a ball of dividing cells, stages that look like a tadpole, etc.) and cannot survive outside the womb until at/or about 6 months gestation (the start of the third trimester) – and **even then**, prior to about 8 months gestation (2/3rds of the way through the third trimester) – **it cannot survive outside of the womb without intensive, ongoing, medical interventions** (neonatal intensive care).

While doctors calculate gestational age from the first date of the woman's last menstrual period, it is important to recognize that a woman cannot be pregnant before she ovulates (before the sperm CAN meet the egg), which is generally 2 to 4 weeks after the date of her last period. Because they count from your last menstrual period (LMP), the length of pregnancy is calculated as 38 to 42 weeks, and pregnancy is treated as essentially 10 months long (instead of its actual 9 months, or 34 to 38 weeks, which is the physical reality). Also, each trimester (one third) is calculated as a little longer than 13 weeks.[210]

Religious Tolerance.org documents the gestational stages. At:

---

210 https://www.plannedparenthood.org/learn/pregnancy/pregnancy-month-by-month

About 3 days after conception: The zygote now consists of about 16 cells and is called a morula (a.k.a. pre-embryo). It has normally reached or exited the fallopian tube and entered the uterus.[211]

5 days or so after conception: The grouping of cells are now called a blastocyst. . . . It has traveled down the fallopian tubes and has started to attach itself to the endometrium, the inside wall of the uterus. The cells in the inside of the blastocyst, called the embryoblast, start forming the embryo. The outer cells, called the trophoblast, start to form the placenta. The blastocyst is often referred to as a "pre-embryo."[212]

9 or 10 days after conception: The blastocyst has fully attached itself to the endometrium -- the inner lining of the uterus. Primitive placental blood circulation begins. . . .

> Medical researchers once speculated that if a woman has taken EC (emergency contraception, a.k.a. the "morning after" pill) quickly after unprotected intercourse, *and* it has not prevented ovulation (thus, not preventing conception), then the EC might prevent the blastocyst from attaching to the wall of the womb. However, further research has shown that this third mechanism appears to be impossible. That is, EC acts as a true contraceptive. Many [anti-choice] groups and religious conservatives reject the research findings . . . . Since these groups generally regard pregnancy as having started at conception, they regard emergency contraception as a possible abortifacient. Many routinely refer to it as an actual abortifacient. In spite of manufacturers' objections, and the findings of research scientists, the U.S. federal government still requires EC packaging to state that preventing

---

[211] http://www.religioustolerance.org/abo_fetu.htm
[212] ibid

implantation is still a possibility,"[213]

but this is contrary to science.

> **12 days or so after conception:** The blastocyst has started to produce unique hormones which can be detected in the woman's urine. This is the event that all (or almost) all pro-choice groups and almost all physicians (who are not conservative Christians) define to be the start of pregnancy. If instructions are followed exactly, a home-pregnancy test will reliably detect pregnancy at this point, or shortly thereafter.[214]

> **13 or 14 days after conception:** A "*primitive streak*" appears in the embryo. It will later develop into the . . . spinal column. This is the point at which spontaneous division of the blastocyst – the process by which identical twins are developed – is no longer possible. The pre-embryo is now referred to as an embryo. It is a very small cluster of undifferentiated cells at this stage of development. It has no functioning brain; it has no internal organs; it is not conscious at this stage, or for many months afterwards.[215]

Whether the embryo is a human person at this state of development is a hotly contested debate:

- Most in the anti-choice community say that it has been a person since conception. They often refer to pre-embryos and embryos as "babies."

- Most in the pro-choice community refer to it as an

---

[213] ibid
[214] ibid
[215] ibid

embryo and believe that personhood is only attained much later in gestation – perhaps at birth.

This lack of agreement generates most of the conflict, heat, and anger over women's abortion access.[216]

> **3 weeks**: The embryo is now about 1/12" long, the size of a pencil point. It most closely resembles a worm – long and thin and with a segmented end. An early vein begins to pulse at about 18 to 21 days after conception, but no internal organs have formed. Before this time, the woman might have noticed that her menstrual period is late; she might suspect that she is pregnant and conduct a pregnancy test. In the U.S., about half of all pregnancies are unplanned. About half of these are terminated by an early abortion.[217]

> **4 weeks [1 month]**: The embryo is now about 1/5" long. It looks something like a tadpole. The structure that will develop into a head is visible, as is a noticeable tail. The embryo has structures like the gills of a fish in the area that will later develop into a throat.[218]

> **5 weeks**: Tiny arm and leg *buds* have formed. . . . The face *"has a distinctly reptilian aspect . . . the embryo still has a tail and cannot be distinguished from pig, rabbit, elephant, or chick embryos .* . . ."[219]

> **6 weeks**: The embryo is about 1/2" long. The face has two eyes, one on each side of its head. The front of the

---

[216] ibid
[217] http://www.religioustolerance.org/stages-of-human-embryo-and-fetal-debelopment.htm
[218] ibid
[219] ibid

face has *"connected slits where the mouth and nose eventually will be."*[220]

7 weeks: The embryo has almost lost its tail. *"The face is mammalian but somewhat pig-like. . . ."* .**The higher functions of the brain have yet to develop, and the pathways to transfer pain signals from the pain sensors to the brain do not exist at this stage of development.**[221]

20 weeks or 4.6 months: Many social and religious conservatives with anti-choice views assert that a fetus can feel pain at 20 weeks. . . . a belief [with] which very few medical researchers agree.[222]

22 weeks or 5 months: 12" long and weighing about a pound, the fetus has hair on its head. Its movements can probably be felt by the mother ["quickening"]. An elective abortion is *usually unavailable* at this gestational age because of state and province medical society regulations, except under very unusual circumstances. The vast majority of fetuses who are born at 22 weeks died or suffered serious health issues. However, half-way through the 22nd week, the fetus' lungs may be developed to the point where it would have a miniscule chance to live on its own. State laws and medical association regulations generally outlaw almost all abortions beyond 20 or 21 weeks gestation.[223]

> "A baby born during the 22nd week has a 14.8 percent chance of survival. And about half of these survivors are brain-damaged, either by lack of oxygen (from poor initial respiration) or too much oxygen (from the ventilator). Neonatologists predict that no baby will

---

[220] ibid
[221] ibid
[222] ibid
[223] ibid

ever be viable before the 22nd week, because before then, the lungs are not fully formed."[224]

Fetal survival rate:

"Most babies at 22 weeks are not resuscitated because survival without major disability is so rare. A baby's chances for survival increases 3 to 4% per day between 23 and 24 weeks of gestation and about 2 to 3% per day between 24 and 26 weeks of gestation. After 26 weeks the rate of survival increases at a much slower rate because survival is high already."[225]

26 weeks or 6 months [beginning of the third trimester]: The fetus 14" long and almost two pounds. The lungs' bronchioles develop. Interlinking of the brain's neurons begins. **The higher functions of the fetal brain turn on for the first time. Some rudimentary brain waves indicating consciousness can be detected. The fetus will probably be able to feel pain for the first time. It has become conscious to some degree of its surroundings. The fetus has become a sentient human life for the first time . . . .**[226]

7 months or 30.5 weeks: 16" long and weighing about three pounds. Regular brain waves are detectable which are similar to those in adults.[227]

As you can see, the potential human life is entirely dependent on the body of its host – and during most of gestation, is not, yet, a human *baby*.

---

[224] ibid
[225] ibid
[226] ibid
[227] ibid

Premature infants survive today, in good numbers, *because* advanced neonatal units offer *intensive* care – that allows the prematurely-born fetus to continue its gestational development outside of the womb.

Depending on the stage of fetal development at which they enter care, NICU units support preterm infants as they finish their fetal development by regulating their body temperature, keeping them safe from microorganisms, regulating and stimulating their breathing, monitoring their brains for hemorrhages, feeding them through tubes when they have not yet developed a sufficient sucking reflex, and much, much more.

Since 91% of abortion procedures[228] in the U.S. are performed before the end of the first trimester (the window in which abortion is available on demand), instead of showing images of what appear to be third trimester fetuses, or even full term neonates, Anti-Choice posters should show a fetus at (or less than) 13 weeks or 3 months gestation – 3 inches long and weighing about an ounce.[229]

Does the Fetus Feel Pain?

The fetus at the end of the first trimester (13 weeks or 3 month) window has just passed from embryo to fetus, and has not yet acquired the brain development to "become conscious" or sensible to pain – at least not in a

---

[228] FoxNews. Fast Facts: U.S. Abortion Statistics. 2003.
http://www.foxnews.com/story/2003/06/17/fast-facts-us-abortion-statistics.html
[229] http://www.religioustolerance.org/stages-of-human-embryo-and-fetal-debelopment.htm

way that is dependent on a human brain – which it has not yet formed in that way. (As an organism, it does not yet have the capacity to be "sentient.")[230]

In fact, it is not until "the 26th week of pregnancy" – fully into the third trimester (well after abortion is *no longer available on demand*) -- that the "fetus becomes sentient," because "only then do its higher brain functions first appear, and the fetus" begins "to some degree" to "become aware of its environment."[231]

Altered images of the gestational age and size of the fetus have been a staple of the Anti-Choice strategy to reframe the abortion debate as the murder of the innocents[232] or as a holocaust of the unborn – rendering it difficult to remember the gestational reality and not the *Photoshopped* propaganda.[233] In the framing of the fetus as baby, every attempt is made to accent the perceived humanness of aborted tissue, to increase the sizing of the images, to downplay parts of the fetus that at various stages do not yet look "human," and to represent it as independent of the girl/woman who must gestate, carry it to (or near) term, and deliver (or be delivered of) it.

In this visual depiction of fetus as fully-developed baby, not only is the physical presence of the girl/woman as incubator absent, but the contextualization of the girl/woman's life is also missing.

Neither the impact of pregnancy on the female body—nor the impact of pregnancy, childbirth, and childrearing on any given mother's social self—is included in this interpretive frame. Unborn *children-to-be* are

---

[230] ibid

[231] http://www.religioustolerance.org/abo_fetu.htm

[232] A reference to the Christian bible story of the murder of infants two years old and younger in Bethlehem in an attempt to exterminate "the Christ" child.

[233] Petchesky 1987

pictured as self-sufficient entities, deserving of (if not parents who want them), at least a chance to be adopted into the spheres of other happy families.

The infinite variability of women's struggles, hopes, and dreams – and of the physical/ emotional/ mental/ financial costs of pregnancy and childcare – disappear in a pronatalist portrait of the happy, healthy, *almost-exclusively-White*, and independent baby, who once born – like children on television sitcoms – is always sweet, clean, and adorable, and conveniently only requires care when it fits the script.

Portraying the fetus, at any given stage of gestation, as larger than life, emancipates the image of the fetus from the girl/woman in whom it is growing, and leads to the interpretation of the autonomous (*yet abortable*) fetus as the victim of the self-serving self-centeredness of the girl/woman who refuses to lend her body for the three quarters of a year it would take to carry it to term – who refuses to *give it* "life"[234] – even to give it away – and thus, takes the life it would have had if she had served it better.

So, women tired of the terrors of the back-alley, and "doctors of conscience"[235] tired of losing patients, fought for the cultural understanding that not all women could (or should), at all stages in their lives, take on the role of becoming a mother. Their persistence raised public consciousness to the place where the Supreme Court granted women their right to privately make their own decisions in the first trimester of an unplanned pregnancy, and to make decisions with their doctors in the event of a problem in the second trimester.

---

[234] Condit 1990
[235] Joffe 1995

However, when the Court rested, the conservative reaction did not, and the narratives it continues to frame in the face of what it constructs as the demise of the traditional family and thereby, the demise of social order as we know it, have not been looked at closely enough.

And while the Pro-Choice narratives of the 1960s were extremely effective in raising public consciousness of the plight (and untimely deaths) of women who received unsafe illegal abortions, there have been no comparably compelling Pro-Choice narrative or visual to counteract the backlash strategy of the Anti-Choice visuals.[236]

Many politicians vote for measures that:

- deny government aid to the poor (including welfare for poor women who choose to carry their babies to term), and that

- affirm parental rights over the rights of minor girls

    o parental approval laws are particularly problematic in regard to abortion, because when very young teen girls get pregnant, a large proportion are actually pregnant by incest (by male relatives, often, their fathers). Requiring a teenage girl to receive permission from her perpetrator, or to carry to term her sibling (the child of her father) – or to carry any child to term, because her parents say so – gives parents rights over a *nearing-adulthood* girl that will affect her across her entire adult lifetime.

While adult, **middle**-class women, in the early stages of pregnancy, still have greater reproductive autonomy than they had in the pre-Roe era, it is apparent that the restrictive legislation passed since Roe affirms patriarchy

---

[236] Condit 1990

and works toward maintaining the family, race, and class status quo.[237]

In their attempt to restrict access to legal abortion, and to turn back its legalization, the Anti-Choice Movement and the Religious Right frame the abortion issue so as to construct an image that casts abortion, and abortion seekers, in the worst possible light.

They present the facts of the law, of abortion procedures, of women's freedom of access, of women's pre-Roe access, and of the "types" of women who obtain or refuse abortions in ways meant to anthropomorphize the zygote/embryo/fetus, to demean as careless or callous the women who end up pregnant unintentionally and use their access to abortion, to frame early termination as murder and late termination as frivolously chosen, and to paint a past in which *pre-Roe* women did not intentionally terminate (or seek to terminate) early pregnancies.

They write and speak as if the *Roe* ruling created abortion – instead of providing safety to women who already would have sought abortion without *Roe*.

They tell **an untrue narrative of** present-day **unrestricted access** in all stages of pregnancy – *by self-centered, narcissistic, career women/ out-of-control suburban teens/ and sexually-promiscuous urban women frivolously, and repetitiously, aborting healthy, well-developed, late-term fetuses* – **as a substitute for** the inconvenience of simply being responsible about **contraception** in the first place – **all the while (incongruously) arguing against (insurance company coverage of) contraception itself.**

They have also erroneously constructed their historical narratives to

---

[237] Saletan 2003

propose a historic, near-universal, anti-abortion stance in Western culture across time.

To hear them tell, abortion began with *Roe*, and would end tomorrow if *Roe* were overturned. Then they:

- frame their visuals of a larger-than-life, gestationally-mature fetus

- add a narrative of a woman who regrets her abortion decision

- then have her display her remorse through a Christian "salvation" experience (repentance).

This movement seeks to turn back the clock on women's rights, to return us all to a world in which women were under the educational and economic domination of men who – as their fathers and husbands – were their owners; a world in which women were chaste outside of marriage and were "barefoot and pregnant" inside marriage – in the "kitchen" of domestic and sexual servitude.

Within their religious beliefs, there is nothing else they can see.

- With a God who wants women perpetually pregnant and under submission to human males

- Who invests an immortal human soul in the fertilized, two-celled, zygote

- Which zygote has rights equal to the rights of the girl or woman in whose womb it may implant

- With a false history of a Christian nation, with no abortion, and with Christian founders

    o who only cared that they themselves not be persecuted for their Christian faith (back in Europe), (*rather than created a pluralist democracy that allows all to follow their own religious conscience and traditions)*

- o and "discovered" by a Christian explorer who was enlightened by faith to the fact that the world was round,

    - and who did "not" commit genocide on Hispaniola, wiping out the indigenous population within two years....

- With a global history in which God created the world – and humankind – just a few thousand years ago –

    - o placed each race separately on its own continent –

    - o and instituted marriage (both monogamous and polygamous) as a heterosexual and male-dominated "sacrament"

- With a sexual ethic that all acts of sex must be potentially reproductive ("open to life"[238]) – and therefore, must consist only of penile-vaginal intercourse without contraception or withdrawal

Within this worldview, they could do no other than to:

- Oppose all same-sex relationships, no matter how committed or legally-united

- Oppose all expressions of gender nonconformity

- Oppose all sex outside of marriage

- Oppose all marital sex that involves contraceptive intervention or that could not lead to conception (i.e. oral, anal, etc.)

- See the hand of God in each conception that takes place –

    - o even those that happen by rape or incest –

---

[238] Pope Paul VI. 25 July 1968. Humanae Vitae: On the Regulation of Birth. Vatican City: Vatican.

- o even those that threaten the actual, physical life of the mother –

- o even those where carrying to term will allow the newborn to suffer horribly, then die

  - *"Everything happens for a reason." "He never gives you more than you can bear." "Who are we to question God?"*

- Oppose all cultural shifts that enable women to become self-sustaining economic units and to live out from under the "headship" of a man (husband/father/son)

From that fundamentalist worldview:

- feminism and sexual liberation are the problems tearing at the unraveling threads of an imagined, homogenous, Western, Christian culture, and

- God is a God of judgment, and as such, He will take His "hand of protection" off of the nation that turns from His patriarchal laws,

- and the modern Christian is a soldier in the army of the Lord, fighting to hold the line on cultural decline.

12. CONCLUSION

When the Supreme Court pounded its gavel on *Roe v. Wade*, and the Court rested, the conservative fundamentalist/evangelical religious reaction did not.

Progressives who fought for women/girls to have the right to clean, safe, medical abortions might have thought (for a hot second) that the fight was won, but the Fundamentalists (Catholic *and* Protestant) rallied and gathered as the *Religious Right*, reacting to their fears of the demise of the social order – as they conceive it – and of the "traditional" (male-dominant/female-subordinate) family.

But the need of women and girls for access to affordable, reliable, contraception – and when it fails – to safe, legal, abortion, remains.

And, unfortunately, there are new narratives to be told – global and domestic – about the repercussions of the ongoing lack of safe abortions around the globe and about the consequences of declining access in the United States.

Whether or not *Roe* will ever be overturned, the persistence of those who war for God has "won" entire regions of the United States where it is very difficult for a woman or girl to obtain a safe, legal abortion. In many places in the country, women/girls of all colors, ethnicities, ages, and religious backgrounds face renewed structural barriers to obtaining services: wait times, parental permission restrictions (or court overrides), mandatory counseling, mandatory ultrasounds, lack of clinics, and protesters problematizing access, and expense (lack of insurance coverage, especially for the poor) often magnified by travel time or hotel fees to stay through mandatory wait times).

Without the problems heaped on by new restrictions, upon discovering a pregnancy, women/girls already face their own psychological smorgasbord: their own religious worldviews (*Will their God hate or punish them?*), their relationship (or lack thereof) with the male who impregnated them, their personal estimations of the long-term consequences (*If they keep this pregnancy, what will their life look like? Is there a way to make peace with this timing, this father, this situation, these finances? If they want, will they be able to have a child later?*)

All of this must be wrestled with in a short time – short enough to make a decision – and access services – before that first trimester runs out.

The effective pro-choice narratives of the 1960s[239] – need to be, and are being – joined by the pro-choice narratives of this time.

We need again to raise public consciousness

- of the fact that, though no one "likes" it – women seek abortion in the same approximate proportion of pregnancies, whether or not it is safe and legal

- of the fact that without access to affordable, legal abortions women/girls will (and do) die (cutting their lives short and bereaving their families)

- of the fact that childhood is so fraught for the luckiest of us,

---

[239] Condit 1990

that being "wanted" is a bedrock essential to a decent start toward a productive life

- of the fact that adoption is not an easy catch-all answer for pregnant women and girls

- of the fact that adoption is not an easy catch-all answer for the already half a million U.S. children in foster care, waiting to be adopted

- and of the fact that (generally) no one else (not even the State) wants the responsibility to raise the children women/girls bear

    o as shown by the antipathy of the state toward AFDC (Aid to Families with Dependent Children, a.k.a. Welfare)

And since none of us like abortion, it is important to highlight – again – that **the most sure method of reducing the need for abortion is increased and affordable access to – and accurate (not fear-based) information about**[240] **– birth control.**

CONTRACEPTION – preventing unwanted pregnancies in the first place – is the most effect means of reducing abortion.

Outlawing (or problematizing access to and accurate knowledge about) contraception leads to a dramatic **increase** in unwanted pregnancies, abortions, infanticide, and children who are mistreated by stressed and

---

[240] "Although use of the most effective forms of reversible contraception (i.e., intrauterine devices and hormonal implants, which are as effective as sterilization at preventing unintended pregnancy) (*92*) has increased (*93–95*), use of these methods in the United States remains among the lowest of any developed country (*94,96*), and the percentage of pregnancies that are unintended remains high at approximately 50% (*46,47*)." Pazol,PhD, Karen & Andreea A. Creanga, MD, PhD, & Denise J. Jamieson, MD. 27 Nov 2015.
Abortion Surveillance — United States, 2012. Surveillance Summaries 64(SS10): 1-40. CDC.gov. http://www.cdc.gov/mmwr/preview/mmwrhtml/ss6410a1.htm

overwhelmed parents or cast adrift on the system.

Outlawing abortion does not reduce the overall number of abortions but does lead to a dramatic **increase** in maternal deaths.

According to the U.S. Center for Disease Control (CDC),

> Research has shown that providing contraception for women at no cost increases use of the most effective methods and can reduce abortion rates. Removing cost as a barrier and increasing access to the most effective contraceptive methods can help to reduce the number of unintended pregnancies and consequently the number of abortions performed in the United States."[241]

People are people. They will have sex, inside and outside of marriage. And not all people are (financially, mentally, emotionally, physically) prepared, or able, to be "open to life" with each act of marital – or non-marital – sex.

If we are sincere in caring for life, we will keep the issue of an unwanted pregnancy in the context of the 9 months gestation/18 years of childrearing that we ask from women/girls, when we deny:[242] the morning after pill, a very early medicinal abortion, a first trimester (<13 weeks) surgical abortion, or a second trimester abortion for medical reasons.

If we are sincere in caring for life, we will care about the lives of *already-born* women/girls – and (when pregnancy is too much to bear) not return them to the back-allies for unsanitary, unskilled, dangerous, and maternal-life-threatening resolution of pregnancy.

---

[241] Pazol, PhD, Karen & Andreea A. Creanga, MD, PhD, & Denise J. Jamieson, MD. 27 Nov 2015. *Abortion Surveillance — United States, 2012.* Surveillance Summaries 64(SS10): 1-40. CDC.gov. http://www.cdc.gov/mmwr/preview/mmwrhtml/ss6410a1.htm

[242] Or make access more difficult or expensive

And if we are sincere about reducing abortion, we will (*rather than label methods as abortifacient when they are clinically-demonstrated not to be*) educate about, and promote, effective means of contraception – and rather than fighting not to cover them via health insurance, **we will make them both affordable and readily available – in the U.S. – and around the world.**

And ~ **work*women*** ~ will increasingly contribute to the lofty spires of our cathedrals and to the annals of our literature.

REFERENCES

AEA (Adoption Exchange Association). (2002-2018). *About the Children.* AdoptUsKids.org. https://www.adoptuskids.org/meet-the-children/children-in-foster-care/about-the-children

A&E. (2018). *On This Day 7Feb. 2002 President George W. Bush Announces Plan for "Faith-Based Initiatives."* http://www.history.com/this-day-in-history/president-george-w-bush-announces-plan-for-faith-based-initiatives

Andrew, Ruby P. (24 May 2006). *Child Sexual Abuse and the State: Applying Critical Outsider Methodologies to Legislative Policymaking: Abstract .* UC Davis Law Review, Vol. 39(5). http://ssrn.com/abstract=904100

Arlaine Rockey, J.D., Arlaine. (2003). *Custody Cases: Protecting Children From Child Abuse.* https://protectingourchildrenfrombeingsold.wordpress.com/about/custody-cases-protecting-children-from-sexual-abuse/

Andrew, Ruby. (accessed 24 Aug 2016). *Child Sexual Abuse and the State.* http://papers.ssrn.com/sol3/papers.cfm?abstract_id=904100)

Barry, Brian & Samuel L. Popkin. (1984). *Forward.* in Kristin Luker, *Abortion and the Politics of Motherhood.* Berkeley: University of California Press.

Barry, Kathleen. (2006). *A History of Flight Attendants: Timeline of Flight Attendants' Fight Against Discrimination.* FemininityinFlight.com. http://femininityinflight.com/activism.html

California Courts. (accessed 24 Aug 2016). *Children and Domestic Violence.* http://www.courts.ca.gov/1268.htm

Cindy Dumas, J.D. (25 Aug 2014). In MCMoewe. *Judge: I Gave a Child Molester Custody of His Daughter.*

http://www.dailykos.com/story/2014/8/25/1324443/-Judge-I-Gave-a-Child-Molester-Custody-of-His-Daughter

Cole, George & Stanislaw Frankowski. (1987). *Abortion and Protection of the Human Fetus: Legal Problems in a Cross-Cultural Perspective*. Martinus Nijhoff Publishers. (p.20).

Condit, Celeste Michelle. (1990). *Decoding Abortion Rhetoric: Communicating Social Change*. Urbana, IL: University of Illinois Press.

Contracept.Org. (accessed 24 Aug 2016). *Ineffective Contraception: Withdrawal*. http://www.contracept.org/withdrawal.php

Davis, Evan Grae. (dir.). (2012). *"It's a Girl"* Shadowline Films.

Enriquez, Lauren. (28 Nov 2014). *Myth that 1 in 3 Women Have Abortions Persists Despite Hard Evidence to the Contrary*. LiveActionNews.org. http://liveactionnews.org/myth-that-1-in-3-women-have-abortions-persists-despite-hard-evidence-to-the-contrary/

Faludi, Susan. (1991). *Backlash: The Undeclared War Against American Women*. New York: Crown.

Fetner, Tina. (2001). *Working Anita Bryant: The Impact of Christian Anti-Gay Activism on Lesbian and Gay Movement Claims*. Social Problems. 48(3):411-428. 2001.

FoxNews.com. (17 Jun 2003). *Fast Facts: U.S. Abortion Statistics*. http://www.foxnews.com/story/2003/06/17/fast-facts-us-abortion-statistics.html

Friedan, Betty. (1963). *The Feminine Mystique*. New York: W.W. Norton & Company.

Gazit, Chana & David Steward. (dir.). (17 Feb 2003). PBS. *American Experience: The Pill*. WGBH-TV; www.pbs.org/wgbh/amex/pill/peopleevents

Giertych, O.P., Fr. Wojciech (5 Feb 2013). In Francis X. Rocca. *Why Not Women Priests? The Papal Theologian Explains*. Catholic News Service. National Catholic Reporter. https://www.ncronline.org/news/theology/why-not-women-priests-papal-theologian-explains

Ginsburg, Faye D. (1998/1989). *Contested Lives: The Abortion Debate in an American Community.* Berkeley: University of California Press.

Greenhouse, Linda. (2005). *Becoming Justice Blackmun: Harry Blackmun's Supreme Court Journey.* New York: Times Books. (p. 92)

Guttmacher Institute. (May 2016). *Induced Abortion in the United States.* https://www.guttmacher.org/fact-sheet/induced-abortion-united-states

Haddad, MD, MA., Lisa B. and Nawal M. Nour, MD, MPH. (Spring 2009). *Unsafe Abortion: Unnecessary Maternal Mortality.* Reviews in Obstetrics and Gynecology. 2009 Spring; 2(2): 122–126. http://www.ncbi.nlm.nih.gov/pmc/articles/PMC2709326/

Hall, Katy & Chris Spurlock. (26 Jan 2013). *Worst States for Pregnant Rape Victims* (Infographic). HuffingtonPost.com. http://www.huffingtonpost.com/2013/01/26/pregnant-rape-abortion_n_2552183.html

Heise, Lori L. (1997). *Violence, Sexuality, and Women's Lives.* In Roger N. Lancaster & Micaela di Leonardo. The Gender Sexuality Reader: Culture, History, Political Economy. New York: Routledge. (pp.411-433).

Hern, Warren, M.D., M.P.H., Ph.D. (1995-2010). *Third Trimester Abortion.* http://www.drhern.com/en/abortion-services/third-trimester-abortion.html

JusticeWomen.com. (2010). *Beware Child Protective Services: What Victims, Advocates, and Mandated Reporters Need to Know.* http://justicewomen.com/tips_bewarechildprotectiveservices.html

Kempner, Martha. (21 Jan 2015). *Pope Francis' Remarks About Birth Control 'Methods' Offend Pro-Choice Catholics.* Rewire. https://rewire.news/article/2015/01/21/pope-francis-remarks-birth-control-methods-offend-pro-choice-catholics/

King, M.D., Jeffrey C. (accessed 20 Aug 2016). *Maternal Mortality in the United States: Current Status* (PowerPoint). ACOG.org.

https://www.acog.org/-/media/Departments/Public-Health-and-Social-Issues/Maternal-Mortality-In-The-US.pdf?la=en

Kilbourne, Jean. (2010). In Sut Jhally (director). *Killing Us Softly 4: Advertising's Image of Women*. DVD. Northampton, MA: Media Education Foundation. www.mediaed.org, www.jeankilbourne.com

_____. (2000). In Sut Jhally (director). *Killing Us Softly 3: Advertising's Image of Women*. DVD. Northampton, MA: Media Education Foundation. . www.mediaed.org, www.jeankilbourne.com

Joffe, Carole. (1995). *Doctors of Conscience: The Struggle to Provide Abortion Before and After Roe v. Wade*. Boston: Beacon Press.

_____. (1985). *The Meaning of the Abortion Conflict*. Contemporary Sociology. 14(1):26-29.

Lee, Michelle Ye Hee. (30 Sep 2015). *The Stale Claim That 'One In Three' Women Will Have An Abortion By Age 45*. https://www.washingtonpost.com/news/fact-checker/wp/2015/09/30/the-stale-claim-that-one-in-three-women-will-have-an-abortion-by-age-45/

Luker, Kristin. (1984). *Abortion and the Politics of Motherhood*. Berkeley: University of California Press.

Miller, Casey W. (Feb 2013). *Admissions Criteria and Diversity in Graduate School*. APS News. http://www.aps.org/publications/apsnews/201302/backpage.cfm; https://arxiv.org/pdf/1302.3929.pdf

NCSL.org. (28 Jan 2016). *Parental Rights and Sexual Assault*. National Conference of State Legislators. http://www.ncsl.org/research/human-services/parental-rights-and-sexual-assault.aspx

Nolan, Caitlin. (9 Mar 2016). *Pregnant Through Rape, Women are Forced to Share Child Custody With Their Attackers*. InsideEdition.com. http://www.insideedition.com/headlines/15130-pregnant-through-rape-women-are-forced-to-share-child-custody-with-their-attackers

OBOS (Our Bodies Our Selves). (23 Mar 2014). *The Impact of Illegal Abortion*. http://www.ourbodiesourselves.org/health-info/impact-of-illegal-abortion/

OBOS (Our Bodies Our Selves). (28 Mar 2014/18 May 2016). *History of Abortion in the U.S.* http://www.ourbodiesourselves.org/health-info/u-s-abortion-history

Pazol, PhD, Karen & Andreea A. Creanga, MD, PhD, & Denise J. Jamieson, MD. (27 Nov 2015). *Abortion Surveillance — United States, 2012.* Surveillance Summaries 64(SS10): 1-40. CDC.gov. http://www.cdc.gov/mmwr/preview/mmwrhtml/ss6410a1.htm

PBS.org. (2003). *American Experience: The Pill.* http://www.pbs.org/wgbh/amex/pill/sfeature/sf_history_influences.html

Petchesky, Rosalind Pollack. (1990). *Introduction: Beyond "A Woman's Right to Choose"- Feminist Ideas about Reproductive Rights.*, Ch.1. in Abortion and Woman's Choice. Boston: Northeastern University Press.

_____. (1987). *Fetal Images: The Power of Visual Culture in the Politics of Reproduction.* Feminist Studies. 13(2):263-92.

_____. (1985). *Abortion and Woman's Choice: The State, Sexuality, and Reproductive Freedom.* (Northeastern Series in Feminist Theory). Boston: Northeastern University Press.

_____. (1981). *Antiabortion, Antifeminism, and the Rise of the New Right.* Feminist Studies. 7(2):206-46). 1981.

Pope Paul VI. (25 Jul 1968). *Humanae Vitae: On the Regulation of Birth.* Vatican City: Vatican. http://www.webcitation.org/5xI2Wz6n5

Raymond EG, Grimes DA. (11 Feb 2012). *The Comparative Safety of Legal Induced Abortion and Childbirth in the United States.* Obstetrics & Gynecology. (2 Pt 1): 215-9. PubMed.gov. http://www.ncbi.nlm.nih.gov/pubmed/22270271

Religioustolerance.org. (accessed 20 Feb 2018). *Part 1: Stages of Human Life During Pregnancy from Before Conception to a Two-Week Old Embryo.* http://www.religioustolerance.org/abo_fetu.htm

Religioustolerance.org. (accessed 20 Feb 2018). *Part 2: Stages of Human Embryo and Fetal Development from a Three Week Old Embryo to a Newborn.* http://www.religioustolerance.org/stages-of-human-embryo-and-fetal-debelopment.htm

Richert, Scott P. (8 Mar 2017). *Can a Woman Be a Priest in the Catholic Church? The Reasons for the All-Male Priesthood.* ThoughtCo. http://catholicism.about.com/od/beliefsteachings/f/Women_Priests. htm

Salcido, J.D., Judge DeAnn. In MCMoewe. (25 Aug 2014). *Judge: I Gave a Child Molester Custody of His Daughter.* http://www.dailykos.com/story/2014/8/25/1324443/-Judge-I-Gave-a-Child-Molester-Custody-of-His-Daughter

Saletan, William. (2003). *Bearing Right: How Conservatives Won the Abortion War.* Berkeley: University of California Press.

Solinger, Rickie. (1992). *Wake Up Little Susie: Single Pregnancy and Race before Roe v. Wade.* New York: Routledge.

Stacey, Judith. (1991). *Brave New Families: Stories of Domestic Upheaval in Late Twentieth Century America.* New York. Basic Books.

TheOrderOfTheWhiteFeather. (accessed 24 Aug 2016). *Rape Culture and Statistics.* https://wearawhitefeather.wordpress.com/survivors/rape-culture-statistics/

Think Progess.org. (4 Oct 2012). *47,000 Women Die Each Year From Unsafe Abortions.* https://thinkprogress.org/47-000-women-die-each-year-from-unsafe-abortions-d20eae29f11c#.8p3kqj1sj

U.N. (accessed 20 Aug 2016). *Maternal Health.* United Nations Population Fund. http://www.unfpa.org/maternal-health

U.S. Constitution. (accessed 24 Aug 2016). *U.S. Constitution: First Amendment.* Cornell.edu. https://www.law.cornell.edu/constitution/first_amendment

U.S. Supreme Court. (7 Jun 1965). *Griswold v. Connecticut*, 381 U.S. 479 *(Estelle T. Griswold and C. Lee Buxton v. Connecticut).* https://supreme.justia.com/cases/federal/us/381/479/

U.S. Supreme Court. (S. Ct. 1973). *Roe v. Wade*, 410 U.S. 113, Section IX. https://www.law.cornell.edu/wex/roe_v._wade_1973, https://en.wikipedia.org/wiki/Roe_v._Wade

U.S. Supreme Court. (1992). *Planned Parenthood v. Casey*, 505 U.S. at 860. https://www.law.cornell.edu/supremecourt/text/505/833, https://en.wikipedia.org/wiki/Roe_v._Wade

Warren, James. (10 Jul 1986). *Airline Ends Sex-bias Suit For $33 Million.* http://articles.chicagotribune.com/1986-07-10/news/8602190033_1_flight-attendants-eeoc-discrimination

Wikipedia. (accessed 11 August 2016). *Maternal Death.* https://en.wikipedia.org/wiki/Maternal_death

WHO. (Nov 2015). *Maternal Mortality: Fact Sheet #348.* Media Centre. World Health Organization. http://www.who.int/mediacentre/factsheets/fs348/en/

WHO. (2007). *Unsafe abortion: Global and Regional Estimates of the Incidence of Unsafe Abortion and Associated Mortality in 2003.* 5th ed. Geneva: World Health Organization. http://www.who.int/reproductivehealth/publications/unsafeabortion_2003/ua_estimates03.pdf. In Haddad, MD, MA., Lisa B, and Nawal M. Nour, MD, MPH. (Spring 2009). *Unsafe Abortion: Unnecessary Maternal Mortality.* Reviews in Obstetrics and Gynecology. 2009 Spring; 2(2): 122–126. http://www.ncbi.nlm.nih.gov/pmc/articles/PMC2709326/

Wright Glenn, Amy. (28 Jun 2015). *Ordered to Live With An Abuser: How and Why American Family Courts Fail Children.* PhillyVoice.com. http://www.phillyvoice.com/live-abuser-american-family-courts-fail-children/

Woman's Justice Center. (2010). *The Greatest Escape: Special for Victims of Domestic Violence.* http://justicewomen.com/tips_escape.html

1in3Campaign.org. [accessed] (24 Aug 2016). *Hadleigh.* http://www.1in3campaign.org/written-stories/4030#more-4030

CPSIA information can be obtained
at www.ICGtesting.com
Printed in the USA
LVHW051659011020
667693LV00010B/940